Les Recettes du Petit Déjeuner

Les Recettes du "Petit Déjeuner"

A Breakfast Cookbook from

the Chefs of la Madeleine

Copyright

Acknowledgements
Nos Remerciements

Editor	Kathy A. Dubé
Art Director & Photo Stylist	Noëlle LeDoux
Graphic Coordinator	Alison Daffin Schmiege
Proofreader	Mary Whitmore
Photography	Gustav Schmiege
Food Styling	Brooke Leonard
Contributing Writers	Kathy A. Dubé
	Poppy Sundeen
Final Layout, Color & Prepress	Composite Color

Merci Beaucoup

Many thanks to the following people, without whom this cookbook would not have been so successful.

Photo Location Hosts

Jan Barboglio

Noëlle LeDoux

Remy Schaal for sharing so much of his history

Kristine Ackerman for her detailed recipe testing

Table of Contents
Table des Matières

Les Plats du Brunch
Brunch Dishes

Les Pains et les Pâtisseries
Breads and Pastries

La Belle France

La Belgique

Nord Pas de Calais

La Manche

Luxembourg

Aisne

Picardie

L'Allemag

Fernand Selestat, Alsace

Normandie

Champagne Ardenne

Lor

Remy Hunawihr, Alsace

Luc Poitou, Loire Valley

Ile de France

Bretagne

Frédéric Buxy, Burgundy

Fra C

Fabrice Belfort, Strasbourg

Pays de La Loire

Centre Val de Loire

Serge Le Creusot, Burgundy

L'Atlantic

Bourgogne

La Suiss

Poitou Charentes

Limousin

Auvergne

Rhone Alpes

L'Ita

Jean-Luc Fargues, Basque

Aquitaine

Midi Pyrenees

Golfe de Gascogne

Côte d'Azu

Provence

L'Espagne

Languedoc Roussillon

Mer Mediterranée

LeDoux 08

Introduction

In the countryside of France, breakfast isn't one meal but many. On workdays, it might take the form of a pre-dawn cup of café au lait and bites of baguette spread with fruit confitures, followed much later in the morning by a heartier meal of meat entrées, quiche or pâté. On the weekends, breakfast might consist of special treats from the village pâtisserie or boulangerie – flaky croissants, brioche or sugar-dusted beignets.

Of course, American breakfast traditions are altogether different – something we discovered in 1983, when we opened our first stateside la Madeleine French Bakery & Café. After several bewildering months of adjustment, la Madeleine and our American guests settled like blissful newlyweds into a happy compromise: we kept our cherished French recipes, but adapted them to the American concepts of breakfast and brunch.

In the years that followed, our American guests came to treat la Madeleine as their very own kitchen. They wander in, morning newspaper in hand, pick out their favorite pâtisserie, pour a cup of our rich French Roast coffee and claim their favorite table. They meet friends and colleagues to talk things over before tackling the day's demands. They gather on leisurely weekend mornings for omelets and the luxury of lingering over cups of coffee. It's so much a home away from home, we sometimes greet absent-minded patrons still in slippers.

All of which raises the question: if la Madeleine serves as your own kitchen in the mornings, why this cookbook? Why cook for yourself, when we can feed you at la Madeleine? Well, why indeed? The simple answer is that our guests ask us for our recipes, and because we love you, we oblige.

Naturally, we had to modify our recipes to make them work in your kitchen. You see, our chefs measure the European way: grams instead of ounces, liters in place of quarts. They're also accustomed to cooking and baking in large quantities for our cafés, using recipes that call for hundreds of kilos of flour and mixing bowls as big as bathtubs.

The adaptation of la Madeleine recipes was accomplished in the home kitchen of our editor, Kathy Dubé. It was a challenging and delicious task, involving lots of tasting, laughter and stacks of dirty dishes.

The result is the cookbook you hold in your hands. We hope it will spend many happy years in your kitchen, being splattered with batter, dusted with flour, splotched with coffee and loved. May it be the starting point for quiet breakfasts à deux with the love of your life, for brunches with friends, for family reunions, and for whatever blend of French and American breakfast traditions you adopt as your own.

But please don't take this to mean we no longer expect you to join us for breakfast at la Madeleine. We'll still be brewing your coffee and listening for the scuffle of your slippers in our doorway.

Le Petit Déjeuner pour la Fête des Mères

Café au Lait
Fraises Romanoff
Oeufs à la Coque avec Vache Qui Rit
Petits Gâteaux aux Myrtilles

Le Premier Jour d'Ecole

Chocolat Chaud
Céréales aux Fruits Secs
Pain Perdu Royale

La Fête de la Bastille

Lillet au Citron
Baies au Sirop de Bourgogne
Gaufres
Saucisse

Le Petit Déjeuner du Dimanche

Tisane à l'Orange et au Miel
Poires au Four, Gingembre et Miel
Omelette aux Fines Herbes et Gruyère
Pain au Muesli

Le Buffet du Déjeuner de Noël

Mimosa à l'Orange et Canneberge
Pêches à la Menthe et au Vin Blanc
Oeufs en Cocotte
Crêpes Forestières
Tomate à la Provençale
Bacon au Poivre
Kugelhopf
Brioche Ardennaise

Le Brunch du Mariage

Cocktail du Champagne
Soupe aux Fruits de la Passion
Oeufs Brouillés aux Truffes
Galettes de Pommes de Terre au Boursin
Croissants
Confiture aux Fruit Rouge
Financiers

la Madeleine Chefs

Remy Schaal

In France, boys dream of growing up to be pastry chefs the way American boys dream of growing up to be firemen. Such, at least, was Remy Schaal's perspective, as he watched his uncle pull heavenly treats from the ovens of his bakery in Alsace.

By the age of 16, Remy had begun formal training to fulfill his dream. After earning his toque, Remy baked his way across France, from Paris to Chamonix to Rheims to Strasbourg and back again to Alsace.

It was in Alsace that Remy came across a newspaper classified listing, advertising for a pastry instructor willing to move to the United States. Remy responded and soon found himself in Dallas, Texas, at la Madeleine.

Remy and la Madeleine proved to be a perfect match. His love for traditional French baking, combined with an eagerness to understand the tastes of his new homeland, earned Remy the respect of his colleagues. Over the years, he rose from pastry instructor to chef and food purveyor to his current role as la Madeleine corporate executive chef and director of product development.

At least twice a year, Remy returns to France to refresh his roots by meeting with chefs, attending culinary shows and exploring new French tastes. His dedication to preserving la Madeleine's French authenticity is borne out in the dishes he himself creates and in the creations of the chefs he mentors.

Remy's favorite recipe is the Kugelhopf on page 82. It took him years to perfect his technique, which until the publication of this book, was shared only with other la Madeleine bakers.

Serge Faucon

As a schoolboy in the Burgundy village of Le Creusot, Serge Faucon walked past the town bakery every day. He recalls the heavenly aroma of baking bread and wishing he were inside, pulling the billowy loaves out of the wood-burning oven. For him, bread was more than the staff of life; it was his passion and his calling.

At the tender age of 16, Serge began an apprenticeship in boulangerie and pâtisserie. After seven years of attending pastry school and working in the local bakery, Serge earned his Master of Baking degree. He also earned widespread acclaim as a finalist in a national bread-baking competition.

Meanwhile, Serge's brother, who shared his love of the kitchen, had become a chef in Houston and a friend of la Madeleine's own Remy Schaal. The link resulted in Serge's introduction to la Madeleine and a subsequent position in the bakery.

Today Serge is a la Madeleine chef, working with a full spectrum of menu items, along with his first love, bread.

In addition to bread, Serge has a passion for chocolate. He satisfies both with Pain au Chocolate. The recipe is on page 102.

la Madeleine Chefs

Fernand Erdmann

At 5 a.m., when most of us are still asleep, Fernand Erdmann is already stationed at la Madeleine's wood-burning ovens, overseeing the creation of our daily bread.

Long hours in a bakery are nothing new to Fernand. As an apprentice baker in Selestat, France, he lived in a small apartment above the bakery where he learned his craft. The heavenly smell of fresh bread and pastries permeated his dreams of becoming a professional baker.

After earning his Diplôme Brevet de Compagnon in baking and completing his military service, Fernand honed his skills at a bakery in Alsace, France. A growing fascination with baking in wood-burning ovens inspired him to enroll for specialized training. The seven-month course gave him the expertise required to fulfill another dream, that of living in the United States as a baker for la Madeleine.

Like the dough he prepared each morning, Fernand's career stature steadily rose. Today, he serves as general manager of la Madeleine's boulangerie.

Fernand believes that every kitchen deserves the smell of bread baking in the oven. He urges you to try his recipe for Muesli Bread on page 81.

Luc Beaudet

Many baking enthusiasts' fondest childhood memories began in Maman's kitchen. And so it was for Luc Beaudet. Only his mother's kitchen, unlike yours and mine, was in the Poitou region of France. And the skills he learned at her side included baking such famed French legends as croissants.

The love of baking she inspired in Luc led him into formal training in the art of pâtisserie. After earning a degree, Luc enrolled in Les Compagnons du Devoir du Tour de France, an organization dedicated to touring France and learning the pastry techniques unique to each region.

One might think that seven years crisscrossing the French countryside would satisfy Luc's wanderlust. It did not. He packed up his baking tools and headed for Japan, where he worked for two years as a pastry chef before accepting a similar position in Dallas, Texas, with la Madeleine.

Today, Luc serves as market chef for la Madeleine in Atlanta, Georgia, where he enjoys handing down to his children the lessons of his mother's kitchen.

Luc recommends the recipe for Almond Cake on page 91 as a good baking introduction for your children.

la Madeleine Chefs

Frédéric Cordier

Perhaps what first attracted Frédéric Cordier to baking was the warmth of the ovens. He remembers how they took the chill off winters in his native Burgundy, where he learned to bake under the tutelage of the village pastry chef.

The winters were colder still when he left Burgundy to take a bakery job in Verbier, Switzerland. At his next job, as chef de pâtisserie in Fife, Scotland, even the oven's glow couldn't chase the chill of the moors.

Then, while visiting his brother in Dallas, Texas, Frederic made a life-changing discovery: cold weather is optional. He resolved to make the American Sunbelt his new home, and accepted a position with la Madeleine to open new bakeries in Phoenix.

Today, Frédéric heads la Madeleine's Phoenix kitchen, producing pastries *The Arizona Republic* has deemed the best in Phoenix.

Even in Phoenix, winter mornings can be chilly. Frédéric's favorite warm-up is fresh-baked Lemon Ginger Cake. You'll find his recipe on page 92.

Jean-Luc Debic

Jean-Luc brings the southwestern perspective to la Madeleine — southwestern France, that is. Born in Fargues, near the French-Spanish border, Jean-Luc's palate was awakened at an early age by Basque-influenced cuisine. By the age of 14, he was working summers in nearby restaurants — something he continued to do throughout his formal education as a chef.

After five years in Paris as a chef du partie, Jean-Luc further broadened his horizons by taking a position as a chef in Togo, Africa. Two years later, in 1984, he arrived in Dallas, Texas, where he created soups and sauces for la Madeleine.

Jean-Luc left Dallas in 1987, succumbing to the lure of the Bahamas, where he served as chef for a prominent hotel chain. In 1992, Jean-Luc was invited back to the United States to be la Madeleine's assistant director of production.

Lucky for us he accepted. Lucky for you, he contributed his flair for robust flavors to this cookbook.

Jean-Luc is particularly proud of the Basquaise Omelet recipe on page 36. This recipe is one of his favorites from the Basque region of France and he particularly likes it made with both hot and sweet peppers.

la Madeleine Chefs

Fabrice Locatelli

His lifelong career in food preparation began as a small child, when Fabrice was assigned the cow-milking chores on his family farm near Belfort, France. As soon as he was big enough to wield an axe, Fabrice began chopping wood with his father, taking periodic breaks to pick wild mushrooms, nuts and berries for his mother to use in her cooking.

When Fabrice was 14, his sister and her husband opened a bakery near their family home. Preferring a cozy kitchen to bitter cold woods and bread pans to an axe, Fabrice joined their enterprise as a baker's apprentice. Four years of learning his art paid off with first place on the baker's exam.

After completing his military service, Fabrice worked with the town's elder bakers, learning cherished recipes and centuries-old techniques at their sides.

The knowledge served him well at his next position, baking for the Palace in Monte Carlo. Fabrice's reputation traveled, resulting in a job offer from a bakery in Houston, Texas. In 1995, Fabrice joined la Madeleine, where he currently serves as general manager of the home kitchen.

Fabrice has a special fondness for the Walnut & Dried Apricot Cake recipe on page 94. It reminds him of how his mother baked with the walnuts he gathered for her as a child.

Les Boissons, Fruits et Cèrèales

Beverages, Fruits & Cereals

Coffee with Hot Milk

Hot Chocolate

Sweet Orange Tisane

Iced Ginger Tea

Orange Cranberry Mimosa

Champagne with Peaches

Champagne Cocktail

Pernod & Water

Lillet with Lemon

Peaches with Mint & White Wine

Strawberries Romanoff

Roasted Grapefruit

Berries in Burgundy Syrup

Oranges & Raspberries in Champagne

Melon with Port

Rhubarb & Apple Compote

Cold Passion Fruit Soup

Baked Pears with Ginger & Honey

Strawberry & Raspberry Jam

Granola

Muesli

Escaoutoun

In the French countryside, nature rules. Life moves along in rhythm with the seasons. This is particularly evident during the summer fruit harvest, which is celebrated by eating one's fill of fresh fruit at the peak of ripeness. Indeed, just-picked fruit is so cherished that it is served unadorned for dessert as well as for breakfast and lunch.

Here in the United States, where we've become accustomed to the year-long availability of just about everything, la Madeleine still subscribes to seasonality and suggests you consider it when choosing which of our fruit recipes to prepare.

Cereal, as well as fruit, is viewed differently in France than it is in the United States. It's less likely to come from a colorful cardboard box than from a family recipe. The French, like our Swiss neighbors, often serve a blend of toasted whole grains with fresh or dried fruit.

Of course, what one drinks in the morning is as important as what one eats. Coffee is an essential part of the French breakfast, with tea and chocolate as close seconds.

When la Madeleine introduced our robust French Roast coffee in America, guests were delighted with its full-bodied flavor. They begged us to sell them the beans, so they could brew it in their own homes. Naturally, we complied. Still, many of them couldn't duplicate the flavor they'd come to love. If you are among them, you might want to take note of the following coffee-brewing tips:

1) Freshness is key. You can store coffee in a cool, dry, dark place for up to 2 weeks. If you plan to store it longer, freezing is advised.

2) Clean your coffee maker well and often. The oily residue that collects becomes rancid over time and affects taste.

3) Rinse filter papers in hot water to remove bits of loose pulp and to rid white papers of any bleaching agents used in their manufacture.

4) Use cold water, preferably filtered. If using tap water, let the faucet run for a while to remove water that's been sitting in the pipes.

5) Warm the pot before you start brewing by rinsing it with warm water.

6) Use 2 tablespoons of ground coffee for each 6 ounces of water. Most automatic drip coffee makers consider 5 ounces to be a cup, so adjust your measurements accordingly.

*L*est you get the impression that coffee (along with wine, of course) is the only important beverage in France, we'd like to point out the popularity of tea. In fact, France is home to many world famous tea parlors, including one that predates the crowning of Napoleon.

Here are a few tips every tea lover should note:

1) Pre-warm your steeping pot by filling it with hot water. Let it sit for a bit, then drain and place in a slightly warm oven.

2) Start your tea with cold water; filtered water is best. If using tap water, let it run for a bit to clear the pipes.

3) Boil the water in a glass, enamel or stainless steel pot. Aluminum and unlined copper pots can add a metallic flavor to the water.

4) Heat the water just until it reaches a rolling boil. If you boil it too long, the water loses oxygen, causing the tea to taste flat.

5) Tea experts suggest brewing Western teas in glass or ceramic pots and Asian teas in ceramic or enamel.

6) Into the warmed teapot, place 1 teaspoon of tea leaves per cup, plus an extra for the pot. Use a mesh infuser or tea ball.

7) If you have a tea cozy, place it over the pot to increase the temperature, which helps extract the maximum flavor from the leaves. If you don't have a tea cozy, try a thick towel.

8) Steep 3 to 5 minutes. The more delicate teas may take longer than the strong ones.

Coffee with Hot Milk

4 cups whole milk

4 cups hot la Madeleine
French Roast coffee

Hot Chocolate

8 ounces semi sweet chocolate, chopped

1 cup heavy cream

½ vanilla bean split horizontally

6 cups whole milk

¼ cup Cognac (optional)

½ cup heavy cream, lightly whipped
(optional)

3 teaspoons cocoa powder
(optional)

Coffee with Hot Milk
Café au Lait

Café au Lait prevails as a traditional part of every French breakfast. Most of our chefs recall sitting at the kitchen table, sipping Café au Lait from a bowl or large mug. Their delicious steamy morning beverage gradually increased in coffee to parts of milk and sugar, but their Café au Lait remains a staple.

Place the milk into a medium-sized saucepan and heat over medium heat until tiny bubbles form around the edge of the milk.

Add the hot coffee and mix well. Pour into large cups or café au lait bowls.

Makes 8 cups

Easy

Hot Chocolate
Chocolat Chaud

One sip and you will understand why hot chocolate is almost as popular in France as coffee. European hot chocolate calls for bar chocolate rather than cocoa powder, which makes the taste so much richer. Add some Cognac and indulge. Who said hot chocolate was just for children anyway?

Place the chocolate in a medium saucepan. Set aside.

Combine the cream and the vanilla bean in a small saucepan and bring to a boil over medium heat. As soon as the cream comes to a boil, remove the vanilla bean. Immediately pour the hot cream over the chopped chocolate. Stir the mixture with a wooden spoon until the chocolate is completely melted.

In a separate medium saucepan, bring the milk just to a boil over medium heat. Add the optional Cognac and stir.

Divide the chocolate mixture among 6 cups, then top with the hot milk. Whisk the hot chocolate until frothy.

Top with the lightly whipped cream and dust with cocoa if desired.

Serves 6

Easy

If you like your coffee sweetened, add "Peruche" natural cane sugar from France

Sweet Orange Tisane
Tisane à l'Orange et au Miel

Calming and therapeutic, a tisane is simply an herbal tea. Use various herbs to accomplish different cures. Use sage to calm a sore throat, verbena or lime blossom tea to help you sleep, and peppermint tea to aid digestion.

Combine the herbs and the water in a medium saucepan and bring to a boil over medium heat. Add the orange peel, vanilla bean and honey. Remove from the heat, cover and let stand for 5 to 10 minutes. Strain the tisane and serve warm.

Makes 1 quart

Easy

Iced Ginger Tea
Thé Glacé au Gingembre

Mon Dieu! What a refreshing take on ordinary iced tea!

Slice the ginger horizontally into thin pieces. Combine the ginger, water, honey, sugar and lemon peel in a medium saucepan and bring to a boil over medium-high heat. Stir until the sugar is dissolved.

Remove the tea from the heat and let it stand for 45 minutes. Using a slotted spoon, remove the ginger root and the lemon peel. Pour the tea into a pitcher and stir in the fresh lemon juice.

Serve over ice in a tall glass garnished with fresh mint leaves.

Makes 1 ½ quarts

Easy

Ⓑ

Sweet Orange Tisane

5 to 6 fresh herb branches, such as sage, verbena, lime blossom or peppermint

1 quart water

1 6-inch strip organic orange peel

½ vanilla bean split horizontally

1 tablespoon honey

Ⓑ

Iced Ginger Tea

1 4-inch piece fresh ginger root, peeled

6 cups water

½ cup honey

½ cup sugar

peel of 2 organic lemons

1 cup fresh lemon juice

fresh mint leaves, for garnish

Tisanes do not contain caffeine like tea.

Orange Cranberry Mimosa

2 cups fresh orange juice

1 cup cranberry juice

1 bottle brut Champagne, chilled

8 organic orange slices

Champagne with Peaches

1 peach, peeled and sliced

2 cups peach juice

1 bottle brut Champagne, chilled

Orange Cranberry Mimosa
Mimosa à l'Orange et Canneberge

To turn a typical Sunday brunch into a more festive occasion, just add Champagne! Besides the striking presentation, as the crimson cranberry juice joins the orange juice, it adds a unique flavor and depth to the standard Mimosa.

Divide the orange juice evenly among 8 Champagne glasses. Slowly pour the cranberry juice over the orange juice. Top with Champagne and garnish with orange slices.

Serves 8

Easy

Champagne with Peaches
Champagne aux Pêches

This recipe is a variation of the classic Mimosa and can be adapted to any fruit combination. Try it with mangoes, berries with citrus juice or apricots. Just be sure to have plenty of Champagne on hand because your guests will want refills.

Drop a peach slice into the bottom of each of 8 Champagne glasses; divide the peach juice evenly between the glasses. Fill the glasses with Champagne and serve immediately.

Serves 8

Easy

Layering the juices makes this Mimosa truly exciting!

Champagne Cocktail

Cocktail du Champagne

Is it possible to have too much Champagne at your table? We don't think so! This is not a new recipe, but sometimes the classics remain the best.

Sprinkle each sugar cube with 2 dashes of bitters. Place 1 sugar cube into each of 6 Champagne glasses. Pour 1 teaspoon of Cognac over the sugar cube. Add 1 tablespoon of Grand Marnier to each glass. Fill the glass with Champagne and garnish with the orange peel.

Serves 6
Easy

Pernod & Water

Pastis

Pernod is an aniseed-flavored liquor that has been around since the late 1700s. Pastis is very popular at the sidewalk cafés of Montmartre where the artists and writers gather for happy hour or l'Heure Verte as it is called in France. l'Heure Verte, or the Green Hour, refers to the green color of Pernod.

Fill 2 tall glasses halfway with ice cubes. Divide the Pernod equally between each glass and fill to taste with water. Garnish each glass with a twist of lime. The mixture will turn cloudy when you add the water.

Serves 2
Easy

Bitters were developed in the 1800s as an aid to digestion.

Champagne Cocktail

6 sugar cubes

12 dashes Angostura bitters

6 teaspoons Cognac

6 tablespoons Grand Marnier

1 bottle brut Champagne, chilled

6 strips organic orange peel

Pernod & Water

ice cubes

6 ounces Pernod

water, to taste

2 lime twists

Lillet with Lemon
Lillet au Citron

Ⓑ
Ⓑ
Ⓑ

Lillet with Lemon

¼ cup superfine sugar

¼ cup fresh lemon juice

1 cup white Lillet

soda water, chilled

Lillet is a French apéritif, made in the town of Podensac, from Bordeaux wine accented with oranges, honey, fresh mint and spices. Serve chilled with a lemon or orange twist for a refreshing summer drink or before a meal to heighten the appetite.

Combine the sugar and lemon juice in a small saucepan. Bring to a boil over medium heat, stirring until the sugar is dissolved. Refrigerate until needed.

Fill 2 tall glasses with ice; add ½ cup of the Lillet and 1 to 2 tablespoons of the lemon syrup to each glass. Top with soda water and stir.

Serves 2

Easy

Find Lillet in any good liquor store; it is worth the search.

*Peaches with Mint &
White Wine*

½ cup granulated sugar

¾ cup water

1 bunch fresh mint

6 ripe peaches

1 cup dry white wine, such as Pinot
Blanc

Peaches with Mint &
White Wine

Pêches à la Menthe et au Vin Blanc

The flavors of the mint and the wine enhance even frozen peaches, making this a great part of a breakfast celebration at any time of the year. To easily peel fresh peaches, drop the peaches into a pot of rapidly boiling water for 10 to 15 seconds, remove with a slotted spoon and put into a bowl of ice water. Use a small paring knife to remove the peel.

Combine the sugar and water in a small saucepan. Bring to a boil over medium-high heat, stirring until the sugar is dissolved. Add ¾ of the mint (whole leaves) to the syrup, reserving the best leaves for garnish. Set aside.

Peel the peaches and place them in a medium saucepan. Pour the warm mint syrup over the peaches. Bring the peaches to a simmer over medium heat and simmer for 5 minutes. Let the peaches cool in the syrup.

After the peaches are cool, remove them from the syrup with a slotted spoon and set aside. Bring the syrup back to a boil and boil until the syrup is reduced to ¼ of a cup, about 7 minutes. Let the syrup cool to room temperature and then discard the mint. Add the wine and refrigerate until ready to serve.

Cut the peaches into wedges and arrange decoratively in 6 soup plates. Divide the syrup evenly over the peaches and garnish with the remaining mint.

Serves 6

Easy

White peaches will add a very elegant note.

Strawberries Romanoff

Fraises Romanoff

½ cup sour cream

3 tablespoons brown sugar

1 tablespoon Cognac

½ cup heavy cream

3 tablespoons granulated sugar

4 cups (2 pints) fresh strawberries

Roasted Grapefruit

Pamplemousse Rôti

1 grapefruit, preferably Ruby Red

2 tablespoons brown sugar, or to taste

dash cinnamon

2 teaspoons honey, or to taste

Strawberries Romanoff

Fraises Romanoff

Strawberries Romanoff has been a la Madeleine favorite for years. The subtle tanginess of the Romanoff sauce brings the flavor of the strawberries to life. Make sure that your berries are as fresh and ripe as possible; they should be firm but not hard and have a distinct berry aroma.

Mix the sour cream, brown sugar and Cognac together in a medium bowl.

In a separate bowl, whip the cream with a whisk or an electric mixer until it starts to thicken. Add the granulated sugar and whip until thick.

Using a rubber spatula, fold the cream carefully into the sour cream mixture until well blended.

Just before serving, rinse the berries and trim off the green stems with a sharp paring knife.

Put the berries into stemmed wineglasses and top with the Romanoff sauce.

Serves 4   Easy

Roasted Grapefruit

Pamplemousse Rôti

This recipe will turn even the most bitter grapefruit cynic into an enthusiast.

To keep the grapefruit halves from rolling, cut a small slice off the bottom and top of each grapefruit. Cut the grapefruit in half horizontally. Remove all the seeds. Using a grapefruit knife or a sharp paring knife cut along the white membranes to separate the sections. Cut along the outside to free the sections from the rind. Mix the brown sugar and cinnamon together in a small bowl.

Place the grapefruit halves on a baking sheet and top each grapefruit with half of the honey. Then sprinkle each half evenly with the brown sugar and cinnamon mixture.

Broil until the sugar is caramelized, about 5 minutes.

Carefully put the grapefruit into a cereal bowl and serve immediately.

Serves 2   Easy

Rinse the berries before you hull them so they don't become soft.

Berries in Burgundy Syrup

Baies au Sirop de Bourgogne

As you know, table presentation is everything to the French. This fruit dish, with all the different colors, makes a vibrant presentation on any table. You can use any combination of fresh berries; all the flavors blend well with the Burgundy.

Split the vanilla bean in half lengthwise.

Combine the split vanilla bean pieces, wine, sugar and lemon juice in a large saucepan. Bring the mixture to a boil, then lower the heat to a simmer and simmer for 5 minutes or until the sugar is dissolved.

Refrigerate the syrup until cool.

Rinse the berries and pick out any damaged fruit. Trim the green stems from the strawberries with a sharp paring knife. If the strawberries are large, cut them in half. Put the berries into a large bowl, preferably glass, and pour the wine syrup over the berries. Let the berries macerate for at least 2 hours before serving.

Divide the berries evenly among 8 wineglasses or glass bowls, and then pour ¼ cup of the wine syrup over each serving. Garnish with fresh mint.

Serves 8

Easy

Ⓑ
Ⓑ
Ⓑ

Berries in Burgundy Syrup

1 vanilla bean

1 bottle dry red Burgundy

¾ cup granulated sugar

2 tablespoons fresh lemon juice

½ pint (1 cup) red raspberries

½ pint (1 cup) blueberries

½ pint (1 cup) blackberries

1 pint (2 cups) strawberries

fresh mint for garnish (optional)

As the wine simmers, the alcohol in the wine evaporates leaving just the flavor.

Oranges & Raspberries in Champagne

8 organic Navel oranges

1 pint fresh raspberries

1 bottle Champagne or sparkling wine, chilled

Oranges & Raspberries in Champagne

Oranges et Framboises au Champagne

This is another easy fruit recipe that is very festive. Use Navel oranges, so you won't have to seed them. Remember that oranges are sweetest in the winter, which makes it the perfect time to enjoy this recipe.

Use a sharp paring knife to peel the oranges. Keep the knife under the membrane but as close to it as possible to remove without cutting away too much of the orange. Then divide the oranges into sections. You should have clean sections without any trace of the white bitter membrane. Place the oranges in a colander and put the colander on a plate to catch the juices. The oranges will retain their shape better this way. Refrigerate until ready to use.

Rinse the raspberries and discard any bruised fruit.

Place the oranges and raspberries in a glass bowl or in individual wineglasses.

Pour the Champagne over the fruit at the table.

Serves 8

Easy

Try this with other citrus fruits such as tangerines or Ruby Red grapefruit

Melon with Port
Melon au Porto

This recipe is extremely simple to prepare, but the flavor it offers is far from simple. For another classic melon combination, wrap melon wedges with slices of thinly sliced prosciutto or Jambon de Bayonne.

Cut the melons in half and remove the seeds with a spoon. Scoop out the melons with a melon baller, being sure not to go into the rind. Arrange the melon balls in a glass bowl. Pour the Port over the melon balls and let them macerate for 1 hour before serving.

Garnish with fresh mint leaves.

Serves 4 to 6

Easy

Ⓑ Ⓑ

Melon with Port

1 ripe cantaloupe

1 ripe honeydew

¾ cup tawny Port

fresh mint leaves for garnish

Rhubarb & Apple Compote
Compote de Pommes et Rhubarbe

Rhubarb is one of the first signs of spring in France. To make this dish, choose the thinnest, brightest red stalks of rhubarb you can find. Peel the rhubarb like you would a stalk of celery. Use tart cooking apples like Granny Smith or Jonathan that stand up to the intense flavor of the rhubarb.

Combine the sugar, orange juice, rhubarb and apples in a large saucepan. Bring to a simmer and cook, covered, over medium-low heat for 15 minutes or until the rhubarb and the apples are tender. Be careful not to overcook since the rhubarb will get stringy.

Remove from the heat and add the raisins. Adjust the sugar to taste, since rhubarb can be very tart. Serve warm or cold.

Serves 6

Easy

Ⓑ Ⓑ

Rhubarb & Apple Compote

½ cup granulated sugar, or to taste

½ cup fresh orange juice

2 pounds rhubarb (about 3 cups) trimmed, and cut into 1-inch pieces

6 Granny Smith apples (about 5 cups) peeled, cored and thinly sliced

¼ cup golden raisins

Try Craisins (dried cranberries) instead of golden raisins.

Ⓑ
Ⓑ
Ⓑ

Cold Passion Fruit Soup

16 fresh mint leaves, plus extra
for garnish

10 strawberries, cleaned, hulled
and sliced

2 bananas, sliced

2 cups passion fruit nectar

2 cups fresh orange juice

2 tablespoons superfine sugar, or to taste

Cold Passion Fruit Soup

Soupe aux Fruits de la Passion

This light, refreshing soup is a wonderful prelude to a summer brunch. It will also brighten up a winter breakfast since the ingredients are available all year long. Enjoy it whenever you want to infuse your morning with fruit flavors and colors.

Roll the mint leaves into a tight cylinder and slice into strips. Combine the mint, strawberries and bananas together in a large glass bowl. Pour the juices over the fruit and add the sugar. Mix well and refrigerate for 1 hour before serving. Adjust the sugar to taste.

Divide the soup among 4 soup bowls and garnish with fresh mint leaves.

Serves 4

Easy

Find passion fruit nectar at the health food market.

Baked Pears with Ginger and Honey

Poires au Four, Gingembre et Miel

We've tried this recipe with different varieties of pears: Bosc, Anjou, Bartlett. The pears were equally delicious, and all that really matters is that the pears are at the same stage of ripeness. Riper pears will cook more quickly than less ripe pears. This also makes a great dessert, served with softly whipped cream, accented with ginger.

Baked Pears with Ginger & Honey

8 firm but ripe pears, peeled, halved and cored

1 cup light brown sugar

2 teaspoons ground ginger

⅓ cup honey

3 tablespoons fresh lemon juice

2 teaspoons grated lemon peel

3 tablespoons unsalted butter, cut into small pieces

Preheat the oven to 375°.

Butter 1 baking dish large enough to hold all of the pears, or 2 smaller dishes. Arrange the pears cut side down in the baking dish.

Mix the brown sugar and the ginger together in a small bowl and sprinkle over the pears.

Mix the honey, lemon juice and grated lemon peel together in a small bowl and pour over the pears.

Dot the pears with the pieces of butter.

Place the pears into the oven and bake, basting occasionally, until they can be pierced with a fork and the baking juices are thick. This should take about 15 minutes. If the pears are still not tender, continue baking. When the pears are tender, turn them over and bake for 5 more minutes.

Remove the pears from the oven and arrange them on serving plates. Spoon some of the juices over the pears.

Serve immediately.

Pears can be made a day ahead. After baking, leave the pears in the baking pan and cover tightly with plastic wrap. Refrigerate until ready to use. Heat the pears uncovered in a 375° oven for about 15 minutes.

Serves 8

Easy

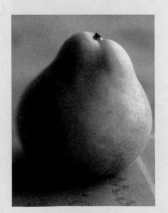

Use a melon baller to scoop out the cores of the pears.

ⒷⒷⒷ

Strawberry & Raspberry Jam

2 pounds ripe strawberries

1 pound raspberries

½ cup water

6 cups + 3 tablespoons granulated sugar

3 tablespoons lemon juice

2 (1.75 ounce) boxes powdered fruit pectin

3 tablespoons Grand Marnier

Strawberry & Raspberry Jam

Confiture aux Fruits Rouge

On a French farm, when everyone has had their fill of fresh fruit in pies, cakes and clafoutis, the rest of the harvest is made into preserves and jams. These jars of preserved fruits are enjoyed throughout the winter. If possible, visit a farmer's market to get the freshest, ripest fruit at the best prices. Your kitchen will get steamy on canning day but the aromas will be great. Perfectly cooked jam falls off a spoon in even sheets. If it is undercooked it will run quickly off a spoon.

Prepare Jars:

Wash and sterilize the jam jars by hand or in the dishwasher. Place the lids in a small pan and cover with water. Just before using, place over high heat and bring to a boil. Turn the heat off and let the lids sit until needed. Wash the rings and set aside. Fill a hot water bath-canning kettle to the correct amount (about 4 inches from the top). Position the rack, cover and bring to a boil slowly while preparing the jam. Set out a wide-mouth funnel, plastic measuring cup or ladle, tongs and a candy thermometer.

Jam:

Wash and dry the berries, removing any damaged fruit. Remove and discard the green stems from the strawberries. Cut the strawberries into quarters if they are large. Place the strawberries and raspberries in a large heavy pan. Add the water and place over medium heat. Bring the mixture to a boil, reduce the heat to medium-low and simmer the berries until soft and reduced to one-half of their original volume. Stir as necessary to keep the fruit from scorching on the bottom. This should take about 10 to 15 minutes. When the fruit has reduced, add the 6 cups of sugar and stir until the sugar is dissolved. Increase the heat and bring the fruit to a boil. Using a candy thermometer to measure the temperature, boil until the jam reaches 221°. Remove the pan from the heat and allow the berries to cool down to 180°.

As the berries cool, mix the pectin, the 3 tablespoons of sugar and the lemon juice together in a small bowl.

Strawberry & Raspberry Jam (suite)
Confiture aux Fruits Rouge

When the jam reaches 180°, stir the pectin into the jam. Place the pan back on the heat, bring the mixture to a boil, stirring constantly, and boil for 3 minutes. Watch so the jam does not boil over and the berries do not scorch on the bottom. Remove the pan from the heat and add the Grand Marnier. Set the jam aside off the heat.

Assemble the warm jars and place them near the jam. Using the funnel, ladle or pour the jam into the jars allowing about ¼- to ½- inch headspace in each jar. Continue until all the jars are filled. Dampen a paper towel with hot water and wipe around the top of each of the jars so that they are completely clean. This ensures a good seal. Place a hot lid on each jar with the sealing compound facing down. Screw a band on evenly using normal pressure. Do not over tighten the ring, just enough to meet with resistance. Place all of the jars on the rack that comes with the canner and gently lower into boiling water. Place the lid on top of the pan and when the water returns to a boil, begin timing. Half-pint jars (1 cup) take 15 minutes of processing. Larger jars take longer. When processing is complete, lift the jars out of the water using the handles on the rack and place the jars on a towel to cool. Do not retighten the rings on the jars. Allow to cool at room temperature for 12 to 24 hours. You will hear popping noises. This means the jars have sealed. To test, after cooling is complete, press the center of the lid. If you hear nothing, the jar is sealed. If you hear clicking, the jar is not sealed. That is not a problem; just store it in the refrigerator and eat that one first. The jars that have sealed can be stored at room temperature for up to 8 months. Be sure to label and date the jars so you remember what you have.

If you do not want to go through the canning process, just fill the jars and seal them as above. Store in the refrigerator and use within 2 months.

Makes 12 (1 cup) jars

Moderate

For best results, use a candy thermometer when making jam.

Granola

Céréales aux Fruits Secs

ⒷGranola

3 cups old-fashioned oats

⅔ cup sliced almonds

½ cup coconut

⅓ cup hulled sunflower seeds

½ teaspoon salt

2 teaspoons ground cinnamon

½ teaspoon ground nutmeg

½ stick unsalted butter

½ cup honey

1 cup mixed dried fruits (raisins, dates, prunes, currants and apricots) in ½-inch pieces

Granola is amazingly easy to make at home. The best part is that you can tailor the mix to your taste; if you don't like raisins, just add more apricots. This recipe is similar to the granola served at la Madeleine. A market with a bulk food section is a good place to shop for the nuts and fruits. You can buy just what you want in any quantity.

Preheat the oven to 325°.

Mix the oats, almonds, coconut, sunflower seeds, salt, cinnamon and nutmeg together in a large bowl.

Melt the butter and the honey together in a small saucepan over low heat.

Pour the butter mixture into the oat mixture and stir until well mixed.

Spread the granola evenly in a large jellyroll pan and bake for 7 minutes. Stir, then bake for another 7 to 8 minutes or until golden brown.

Set the pan on a cooling rack. When the granola is cool, add the dried fruits.

Store in an airtight container for up to 2 weeks.

Makes 6 cups

Easy

 Use different types of honey, like clover and wildflower, for variety.

Muesli

Muesli

1 cup old-fashioned oats

⅛ cup raisins

2 tablespoons sliced almonds

½ cup milk

1 Granny Smith apple, grated

⅛ cup hulled sunflower seeds

2 tablespoons fresh lemon juice

pinch salt

fresh berries, as desired

vanilla yogurt

Muesli

Muesli has a reputation for being "too healthy," but put that notion aside because this is delicious. Muesli has a unique soft texture, but like granola, muesli can be adapted to your personal taste. Don't be shy about adding spices such as cinnamon or nutmeg or adding extra textures and flavors from nuts and dried fruits.

Soak the oats, raisins and almonds in a small bowl in just enough milk to cover. Refrigerate overnight.

Just before serving add the grated apple, sunflower seeds, lemon juice, salt and fresh berries.

Top with vanilla yogurt.

Serves 2

Easy

24   Muesli is also good with chopped and toasted hazelnuts.

Escaoutoun

Escaoutoun

This is the French version of polenta! Chef Jean-Luc ate this for breakfast growing up in the South of France. The only tricky part is slowly adding the cornmeal so that there are no lumps. Confectioners' sugar is a more traditional topping, but maple syrup and cinnamon make a tasty addition.

Combine the salt, sugar and cinnamon with the water in a large saucepan. Bring to a simmer over medium heat and slowly add the cornmeal, stirring constantly with a wooden spoon.

Reduce the heat to low and cook the cornmeal for 20 minutes, stirring occasionally until the cornmeal is thick and smooth.

While the cornmeal is cooking, lightly butter a soup plate or a dish about 1 to 1 ½ inches high. After the cornmeal is thick and smooth, pour it into the prepared plate. Let the cornmeal stand until set, about 10 minutes.

Slice the cornmeal into 3-inch pieces. Roll the pieces in the flour until all the surfaces are lightly coated.

Heat the butter and oil in a medium sauté pan over medium heat until the butter foams. Sauté the cornmeal pieces until brown and crispy on the outside, about 2 minutes per side. Top with confectioners' sugar or syrup and serve.

Serves 6

Easy

Escaoutoun

1 teaspoon salt

2 tablespoons granulated sugar

1 teaspoon ground cinnamon

1 quart water

1 cup cornmeal

flour for dredging

2 tablespoons unsalted butter

2 tablespoons vegetable oil

confectioners' sugar

maple syrup

The oil keeps the butter from burning when sautéing.

Les Notes

Les Oeufs
Eggs

Baked Eggs

Scrambled Eggs with Truffles

Poached Eggs

Herb Omelet with Gruyère

Morel, Ham & Brie Omelet

Basquaise Omelet

Apple Soufflé Omelet

Banana Omelet

Eggs la Madeleine

Soft-Boiled Eggs with Vache Qui Rit

Eggs Meurette

Cheese Soufflé

Spinach Soufflé

In the 1980s, when la Madeleine first opened in Dallas, we had much to learn about U.S. dining habits. One surprise was that Americans think of egg dishes as *breakfast* food; in France, we are more apt to have them for lunch or dinner than breakfast.

What could we say but vive la difference? After all, good food is good food regardless of the hour. With that in mind, we offer up some of our favorite egg dishes for your breakfast enjoyment.

Before you try them, let us share a few basic tips:

1) For best results when cracking an egg, use the edge of a metal bowl. Tap it sharply and decisively in the middle of the egg.

2) When boiling, begin with eggs in cold water. Placing cold eggs into water that's already heated is likely to crack the shell.

3) When poaching an egg, don't break it directly into the simmering water. Break it into a shallow bowl or a teacup and slide it gently into the water.

You'll notice that almost half of the recipes in this section are for omelets. That's because virtually all French chefs (including the ones who wrote this cookbook) have their own ideas of what makes the perfect omelet. Choosing one of their omelet recipes over the others would have proved as inflammatory as Marie Antoinette's cake comment, so we printed the complete spectrum. Each is delicious in its own way.

You'll notice that we have included a couple of — dare we say it — soufflés. It's a word that makes otherwise brave cooks tremble at the prospect of watching their masterpiece deflate like a pricked balloon. But the truth is soufflés are surprisingly easy and not as fragile as they look, making them ideal for delighting guests without courting disaster.

Baked Eggs

Oeufs en Cocotte

This recipe has endless variations and is perfect for a crowd. Instead of using ramekins, you can hollow out small brioches or fill muffin tins with crêpes to make a shell and bake the eggs inside. You can also vary the seasonings. Line the bottom of the ramekin with an orange slice, grated cheese, fresh herbs, mushrooms or whatever strikes your fancy.

Preheat oven to 350°.

Using the melted butter, butter the insides of 8 4-ounce ramekins. Sprinkle the ramekins, rather than the eggs, with salt and pepper, that way the eggs won't have specks in them after they bake. Break an egg into each ramekin and then carefully top each egg with 1 teaspoon of cream.

Place the ramekins on a baking sheet and put into the oven. Bake the eggs in the lower third of the oven for 10 to 15 minutes or until they are set. The yolks may still be soft but the whites should be firm. Sprinkle the chopped chives evenly over the eggs.

Serve in the ramekins with buttered croissants or toast.

Serves 4

Easy

Baked Eggs

2 tablespoons unsalted butter, melted

sea salt, to taste

freshly ground black pepper, to taste

8 large eggs

3 tablespoons heavy cream

2 tablespoons chopped chives

Did you know that chickens with white ear lobes lay white eggs?

Scrambled Eggs with Truffles

Oeufs Brouillés aux Truffes

Truffles make this dish truly luxurious. To enhance the sumptuousness of this dish, keep the eggs soft and creamy by cooking them over indirect heat. For another luxurious variation, cut the tops off the eggshells, fill with plain scrambled eggs and top with caviar. Smoked salmon and chives also lend themselves to these creamy eggs. Simply add salmon and freshly snipped chives to the eggs and cook.

Whisk the eggs with the salt and pepper in a small bowl until well combined. Add the chopped truffles and let stand for 15 to 30 minutes so that the truffles flavor the eggs.

Fill the bottom of a double boiler half-full with water and bring to a simmer over medium heat. Place the egg mixture into the top of the double boiler and place the pan over the simmering water. Stir the eggs gently with a wooden spoon to keep the curds small. As the eggs begin to set, slowly add the butter pieces. It should take about 10 to 15 minutes for the eggs to become soft and creamy.

Adjust the seasonings and serve immediately.

Serves 4

Easy

Scrambled Eggs with Truffles

8 eggs

sea salt, to taste

freshly ground black pepper, to taste

2 black truffles, chopped

2 tablespoons unsalted butter, cut into ½-inch pieces

Serve these eggs with lightly buttered warm toast.

Morel, Ham & Brie Omelet

Omelette aux Morilles, Jambon et Brie

At la Madeleine, we cook our omelets over high heat to give them a toasted look and taste. Some people prefer their omelets cooked slowly with no browning. The French typically eat omelets " baveuse" or soft on the inside. Whichever you prefer, the right pan is essential. A non-stick pan will make it easier to maneuver the omelet while a classic cast-steel pan will brown the eggs better. Whatever type pan you use, you need butter to give the omelet flavor and its characteristic sheen.

Filling:

Melt the butter in a small sauté pan over medium-high heat. Add the ham and sauté for 3 minutes. Add the mushrooms and cook until tender, about 5 minutes. Season with salt and pepper. Remove from the heat and set aside.

Omelet:

Preheat the oven to 200°.

Whisk the eggs thoroughly and season with salt and pepper to taste.

Place a medium sauté pan, preferably non-stick, over medium-high heat and add one-half of the butter. When the butter starts to turn brown, add one-half of the eggs. Stir the eggs constantly with a fork to keep the egg curds as small as possible. When the mixture starts to solidify like custard, stop stirring and let it set for a few seconds. Rap the pan against the burner 2 to 3 times to keep the eggs flat. Reserving a few tablespoons of the ham for garnish, spoon about one-half of the ham mixture and one-half of the Brie pieces down the middle of the omelet.

When the bottom is firm enough to fold but the top is still moist, fold the omelet almost in half with a spatula from the middle to the front of the pan. Tip the pan so that the omelet takes on the curved shape of the pan.

Roll the omelet onto the serving dish, tilting the pan up and away from you. The omelet should roll onto itself with the smooth side on top. Place the omelet in the preheated oven to keep warm while you make the second omelet.

Repeat with the remaining butter, eggs, ham and Brie. Spoon the remaining ham and mushrooms on top of the omelets as garnish.

Serves 2   Moderate

Morels are spring mushrooms.

Filling

2 tablespoons unsalted butter

4 ounces smoked ham, cut into
½- inch cubes

6 ounces sliced morels (can be a combination of any type of mushroom)

sea salt, to taste

freshly ground pepper, to taste

Omelet

6 large eggs

sea salt, to taste

freshly ground black pepper, to taste

1 tablespoon unsalted butter

2 ounces Brie with Herbs,
cut into pieces

2 tablespoons olive oil

1 garlic clove, minced

1 medium onion, peeled and thinly sliced (about 6 ounces)

1 green pepper, seeded, cored and thinly sliced (about 7 ounces)

1 red pepper, seeded, cored and thinly sliced (about 7 ounces)

1 tomato, peeled, seeded and finely chopped (about ⅔ cup)

1 dash Tabasco

½ cup dry white wine

4 slices Jambon de Bayonne or Prosciutto cut into matchsticks (about ½ cup) optional

sea salt, to taste

freshly ground black pepper, to taste

Omelet

2 tablespoons unsalted butter

6 eggs, well beaten

Basquaise Omelet
Omelette Basquaise

This omelet features our variation of "piperade," a pepper and onion mixture traditionally made with Basque peppers. This mix of peppers, onions and ham is savory with a slight sweetness. If you like spicy foods, try making this omelet with hot Italian peppers.

Filling:

Heat the olive oil in a large sauté pan over medium-high heat until fragrant. Add the garlic, onion and peppers and sauté until tender, about 7 or 8 minutes. Toss and stir the vegetables to prevent burning.

Add the tomato, Tabasco, white wine and the optional ham. Toss the mixture together and cook until the peppers are very tender, about 5 to 8 minutes. There should be about 3 cups of filling. Season to taste with salt and pepper. Set aside.

Omelet:

Preheat the oven to 200°.

Heat a 10-inch sauté pan, preferably non-stick, over medium-high heat and add one-half of the butter. When the butter starts to turn brown, add one-half of the eggs. Stir the eggs constantly with a fork to keep the egg curds as small as possible. When the mixture starts to solidify like custard, stop stirring and let it set for a few seconds. Rap the pan against the burner 2 to 3 times to keep the eggs flat. Spoon about one-fourth of the pepper mixture down the middle of the omelet.

When the bottom is firm enough to fold but the top is still moist, fold the omelet not quite in half with a spatula from the middle to the front of the pan. Tip the pan so that the omelet takes on the curved shape of the pan.

Roll the omelet onto the serving dish, tilting the pan up and away from you. The omelet should roll onto itself with the smooth side on top. Place the omelet in the preheated oven to keep warm while you make the second omelet.

Repeat with the remaining butter, eggs and one-fourth of the pepper mixture.

Spoon the additional filling on top of the omelets as garnish.

Serves 2

Moderate

Use a pan with sloping sides when making omelets.

Apple Soufflé Omelet

Omelette Soufflée au Pommes

If you are looking for drama at your breakfast table, this puffy soufflé omelet is just the thing. Make sure everyone is at the table before you serve, since this dish will quickly deflate.

Filling:

Melt 3 tablespoons of butter over medium heat in a large sauté pan. Add the apples, brown sugar, Calvados and cinnamon. Cook, stirring as needed, until the apples are tender, about 5 minutes. Remove the pan from the heat and set the apples aside.

Omelet:

Preheat the oven to 350°.

In a medium bowl, whisk the egg yolks with the granulated sugar and the salt until pale yellow, about 5 minutes. In the bowl of an electric mixer fitted with the whip attachment, beat the egg whites until they form stiff peaks. Add one-third of the egg whites to the yolk mixture and fold until blended to lighten the mixture. Add the rest of the egg whites and fold into the yolk mixture using a rubber spatula with an over-and-under motion, until just blended.

Melt the remaining 3 tablespoons of butter over medium-low heat in a large non-stick ovenproof skillet, making sure that the butter goes up the sides of the pan. Add the eggs and cook over low heat until the edges have begun to puff and the bottom has set and started to brown, about 2 to 3 minutes. Remove the pan from the heat and put it in the oven to bake. The omelet will puff and the top will brown in about 5 to 6 minutes. Remove the skillet from the oven. Spoon the warm apples to the right of the center of the omelet. Slide the omelet onto a serving plate folding the omelet in half on top of the apples. Dust with confectioners' sugar and serve immediately.

Serves 2

Moderate

Filling

6 tablespoons unsalted butter, divided use

2 Granny Smith apples, peeled, cored and sliced very thin

¼ cup packed light brown sugar

1 tablespoon Calvados or Cognac (optional)

½ teaspoon ground cinnamon

Omelet

3 eggs, separated

¼ cup granulated sugar

¼ teaspoon salt

confectioners' sugar for dusting

38 This omelet also makes a great dessert.

Banana Omelet
Omelette Soufflée aux Bananes

Some of the sweetest bananas in the world are grown in Martinique, a province of France in the Caribbean. If you can find small "finger" bananas, this omelet will be even more delicious. Beating the egg whites with a little sugar makes a light meringue which gives the eggs a base to puff to great height.

Filling:

Melt 3 tablespoons of the butter over low heat in a medium sauté pan. Add the bananas and the cinnamon. Cook, stirring as needed until the bananas are soft, about 10 minutes. Remove the pan from the heat and set the bananas aside.

Omelet:

Preheat the oven to 350°.

In a medium bowl, whisk the egg yolks with the granulated sugar, salt and vanilla until pale yellow, about 5 minutes. In the bowl of an electric mixer fitted with the whip attachment, beat the egg whites until they form stiff peaks. Add one-third of the egg whites to the yolk mixture and fold until blended. Add the rest of the egg whites and fold into the yolk mixture using a rubber spatula with an over-and-under motion, until just blended.

Melt the remaining 3 tablespoons of butter over medium heat in a large non-stick ovenproof skillet, making sure that the butter goes up the sides of the pan. Add the eggs and cook over low heat until the edges have begun to puff and the bottom has set and started to brown, about 2 to 3 minutes. Remove the pan from the heat and put in the preheated oven to bake. The omelet will puff and the top will begin to brown in about 5 to 6 minutes. Remove the skillet from the oven. Spoon the warm bananas to the right of the center of the omelet. Slide the omelet onto a serving plate folding the omelet in half on top of the bananas. Dust with confectioners' sugar and serve immediately.

Serves 2

Moderate

Did you know that bananas are America's favorite fruit?

Filling

6 tablespoons unsalted butter, divided use

4 bananas, peeled and sliced thin

½ teaspoon ground cinnamon

Omelet

3 eggs, separated

¼ cup granulated sugar

¼ teaspoon salt

½ teaspoon natural vanilla extract

confectioners' sugar for dusting

Béarnaise Sauce

1 cup dry white wine, such as Riesling or Sancerre

1 shallot, minced (about 1 tablespoon)

½ teaspoon dried tarragon

3 egg yolks

4 tablespoons cold unsalted butter, cut into small pieces

sea salt, to taste

freshly ground black pepper, to taste

Eggs la Madeleine

8 poached eggs (see recipe page 33)

4 croissants, split in half and lightly toasted

1 pound Asparagus in Lemon Oil (see recipe page 73)

Eggs la Madeleine

Oeufs Fait Maison

This is the la Madeleine take on Eggs Benedict: flavorful Béarnaise, from the south of France, buttery croissants and crisp asparagus. Do not make Béarnaise until you are just about ready to eat; it can't be reheated. In case your sauce gets too warm and curdles, whisk in an ice cube for a quick fix. The ice cube cools the butter so that it re-emulsifies. If your sauce turns into something resembling scrambled eggs, you will have to start over.

Béarnaise Sauce:

Combine the white wine, shallot and tarragon in the top half of a double boiler. Place the pan over direct heat and simmer until the mixture is reduced to ⅓ cup, about 10 minutes. Partially fill the bottom half of the double boiler with water and bring to just below a boil. Place the pan with the wine mixture over the water. Add the egg yolks and whisk until the mixture warms and the eggs thicken, about 2 minutes. Keep the mixture moving all the time so the yolks do not curdle.

Add the butter in small pieces, whisking constantly. Do not add more butter before each piece is absorbed. Do not allow the butter to melt completely or the sauce will not be bound together. Remove the top part of the double boiler from the heat as necessary if the sauce becomes too hot. This process should just take 2 minutes or so. When all of the butter is incorporated, remove the sauce from the heat. Whisk again. Season the sauce with salt and pepper to taste. Serve immediately.

Makes 1 cup Béarnaise sauce

To Assemble Eggs la Madeleine:

Split the croissants in half horizontally and lightly toast the cut sides under the broiler. Place each croissant on a serving plate and place 3 to 4 asparagus spears on the bottom half of each croissant. Place 2 poached eggs on the asparagus and top with the Béarnaise sauce. Prop the top half of the croissant against the eggs and serve immediately.

Serves 4

Easy

Store Béarnaise sauce in a Thermos; it will keep for an hour.

Soft-Boiled Eggs with Vache Qui Rit

Oeufs à la Coque avec Vache Qui Rit et Mouillet

All of our French chefs suggested this recipe; they all enjoyed it as children growing up in France. However, in France it is not served for breakfast but for lunch or a light supper. Whenever you try it, remember that it needs to be eaten as soon as the eggs are done. Cold soft-boiled eggs are not a treat! Start the eggs in cold water so they heat slowly and don't crack. A perfect soft-boiled egg has a soft and runny yolk, with a set white.

Place the eggs in a saucepan and cover them with cold water. Bring to a boil over medium heat and boil for 3 minutes from the start of the boil. You need to use a timer or you will have hard-boiled eggs.

Toast the bread, then spread with the cheese. Place the bread under the broiler until the cheese melts. Cut the bread into ½-inch sticks (or mouilletes) and keep warm.

After the eggs are cooked, remove from the water and place in eggcups. Tap the top of the egg with a knife and peel off the top of the eggshell.

Season to taste with salt, freshly ground black pepper and butter.

Dip the toast into the egg yolk.

Serves 4

Easy

Soft-Boiled Eggs with Vache Qui Rit

4 large eggs, at room temperature

4 slices bread

4 ounces Vache qui Rit
(Laughing Cow cheese)

sea salt, to taste

freshly ground black pepper, to taste

butter, optional

A mouillette, pronounced "mooyet," is a toast strip!

Eggs Meurette
Oeufs Pochés en Meurette

The vineyard workers in Burgundy, using the fruits of their labors, created this dish to sustain them during long working hours. Do not be put off by the combination of red wine and poached eggs, as this sauce is the same that is used for Coq au Vin and we all know that is delicious. The wine cuts the richness of the egg; the bacon and shallots add mellow flavors.

Burgundy Wine Sauce

6 slices smoked bacon, diced (about 1 cup)

2 tablespoons diced onions

1 tablespoon minced shallots

2 cups dry red wine, such as Burgundy or Beaujolais

1 tablespoon unsalted butter, softened

1 tablespoon all-purpose flour

To Serve

8 slices baguette (1 inch thick)

1 clove garlic, unpeeled

8 poached eggs (see recipe page 33)

fresh parsley, for garnish

Burgundy Wine Sauce:

Sauté the bacon, onions and shallots in an 8-inch sauté pan over medium heat until the onions and shallots are tender and translucent and the bacon is brown. Using a slotted spoon, remove the bacon, onions and shallots and place on a paper towel to drain. There should be about ½ cup of the bacon mixture. Set aside.

Pour off any excess fat in the pan. Add the wine to the pan and place over medium-high heat. Reduce the wine by half until there is 1 cup remaining. This should take about 10 minutes. Remove the pan from the heat.

In a small bowl, blend the flour and the butter together with the back of a spoon until thoroughly combined.

Place the pan with the wine back over low heat and whisk the butter and flour (beurre manié) mixture into the wine sauce. Continue stirring until the sauce thickens, becomes lighter in color and glossy. Add the reserved bacon, onions and shallots back to the wine sauce. Serve at once or set aside in a warm place while preparing the remainder of the dish.

To Serve:

Close to serving time, slice the bread into 1-inch slices. Toast the bread until golden brown. Cut the garlic in half and rub the cut side over the toast while still warm. The temperature helps release the aroma of the garlic.

For each serving place 2 slices of the toasted baguette in a large, shallow soup plate. Top each piece of toast with a poached egg and divide the hot wine sauce over the eggs, allowing about ⅓ cup per serving. Garnish with parsley if desired.

Serve at once.

Serves 4, makes 1 ½ cups Burgundy Wine Sauce

Moderate

Make this dish in November with the new crop of Beaujolais Nouveau.

Cheese Soufflé

Soufflé au Fromage

Soufflés sound intimidating, but you will be surprised at how easy they are to make. In this recipe, a cheese sauce is lightened with perfectly beaten egg whites. Make sure that your eggs are at room temperature and that your mixing bowl and whisk or beaters are impeccably clean before getting started. Cheese soufflé is perfect for brunch accompanied by a green salad.

Preheat the oven to 400°.

Butter the bottom and sides of a 4-cup soufflé dish. Sprinkle 2 tablespoons of the Parmesan cheese in the soufflé dish. Shake and rotate the dish to coat the interior of the soufflé dish. The pieces of cheese give the soufflé "handles" to climb on during the baking time as well as a nice cheese flavor. Set aside.

In a medium bowl, beat the egg yolks with a whisk until well blended. Set aside.

Melt the butter over medium heat in a large saucepan. Add the shallots and cook until the shallots are tender and translucent, about 3 minutes. Add the flour and whisk to a smooth paste. Add the salt and pepper. Gradually whisk in the milk and cook over low heat, stirring occasionally until the mixture thickens, about 5 minutes.

Remove the pan from the heat. Whisk in a spoonful of the hot cream sauce into the yolks to temper. Then whisk the remaining yolks and cream sauce together until the mixture is smooth. Add the remaining 2 tablespoons of Parmesan and the Gruyère and whisk until the cheese is melted.

Using an electric mixer fitted with the whip attachment, beat the egg whites and the salt together until they form soft peaks. If you tip the mixing bowl the egg whites should not slide. Set aside.

Gently whisk one-fourth of the beaten egg whites into the cheese mixture to lighten it. Carefully fold in the remaining egg whites, using a rubber spatula with an over-and-under motion. Spoon the mixture into the soufflé dish. With the spatula, draw a narrow circle around the top of mixture about 1½ inches from the edge. This will give the soufflé a little "cap" when it is baked.

Place the soufflé in the oven on the lowest shelf and bake for 5 minutes, then reduce the heat to 375°. Bake until the soufflé is puffed and golden, about 25 minutes.

Serve immediately.   Serves 4   Moderate

Substitute Montrachet for the Gruyère for a light supper dish.

Cheese Soufflé

¼ cup grated Parmesan, divided use

4 eggs, separated

2 ½ tablespoons unsalted butter
+ butter for the dish

2 tablespoons minced shallots

3 tablespoons all-purpose flour

½ teaspoon sea salt

1 teaspoon freshly ground black pepper

1 cup milk

¼ cup shredded Gruyère, about 1 ounce

⅛ teaspoon salt

1 tablespoon unsalted butter, softened

2 tablespoons finely grated Parmesan

1 pound fresh spinach,
rinsed and stemmed

4 eggs, separated

1 tablespoon water

3 tablespoons all-purpose flour

⅛ teaspoon sea salt

1 cup milk

½ teaspoon sea salt

¼ teaspoon freshly ground black pepper

pinch of ground nutmeg

Spinach Soufflé

Soufflé aux Epinards

Remember: be sure that your guests are seated at the table when you take your soufflé out of the oven. You want to get kudos for your perfectly puffed creation!

Preheat the oven to 475°.

Butter the bottom and sides of a 4-cup soufflé dish. Sprinkle 2 tablespoons of the Parmesan cheese in the soufflé dish. Shake and rotate the dish to coat the interior of the soufflé dish. Set aside.

Shake the water off the spinach and place the leaves in a medium saucepan. Set the pan over medium heat, cover and steam the spinach until limp, about 5 minutes. You should have about 1 cup of steamed, drained spinach. When cool, squeeze the spinach in a tea towel to get out as much water as possible. Finely chop the spinach. Set aside.

Whisk the egg yolks and water together in a small bowl. Add the flour and whisk until smooth. Set aside.

Using an electric mixer fitted with the whip attachment, beat the egg whites and the salt together until they form soft peaks. Do not overbeat the whites or the soufflé will be dry. If you tip the mixing bowl the egg whites should not slide. Set aside.

Bring the milk to a boil in a small saucepan. Stir about ¼ cup of the hot milk into the egg yolk and flour mixture to temper it. Return all of the egg mixture to the hot milk and whisk rapidly over medium heat until the mixture thickens, about 30 seconds. Cook for 1 minute, whisking constantly.

Reduce the heat to a simmer and season the mixture with the salt, pepper and nutmeg. Add the reserved spinach, stir to incorporate the spinach and remove the pan from the heat.

Pour the spinach mixture into a large bowl and whisk in ¼ of the beaten egg whites to lighten the spinach mixture. Carefully fold in the remaining egg whites, using a rubber spatula with an over-and-under motion.

Pour the mixture into the prepared soufflé mold. With the spatula, draw a narrow circle around the top of mixture about 1½ inches from the edge. This will give the soufflé a little "cap" when it is baked.

Place the soufflé in the oven on the lowest shelf and bake for 8 minutes. Reduce the heat to 425° and bake for another 10 to 12 minutes or until the soufflé is puffed and golden. Serve immediately.

Serves 4

Moderate

Les Notes

Les Plats du Brunch
Brunch Dishes

Quiche Lorraine

Alsacian Onion Tart

Croque Monsieur

Savory Crêpes

Buckwheat Crêpes

Wild Mushroom Crêpes

Shrimp Crêpes

Ham & Gruyère Crêpes

Ratatouille Crêpes

Sweet Crêpes

Waffles

French Toast Royale

Diplomat

Apple Potato Gratin

Potato Cakes with Boursin

Roasted Asparagus with Lemon Oil

Tomato Provençal

Breakfast Sausage

Peppered Bacon

Caramelized Bacon

Salmon Bacon

Le Brunch

B

Brunch

*I*n France, we have no word comparable to the term "brunch," that whimsical amalgam of breakfast and lunch. But while the word isn't part of our lexicon, the concept of a leisurely meal served around noon with dishes such as quiche and crêpes is as French as the Fleur de Lys.

Speaking of crêpes, we'd like to challenge their undeserved reputation for causing last minute disasters. True, it takes a while to get your batter-spreading and flipping techniques down pat, but that ceases to be daunting when you learn that crêpes can be made ahead of time and kept in the refrigerator or freezer. You can work through your trial-and-error phase in private and destroy the evidence.

And while we are separating myth from truth, we must address quiche. Quiche had the mixed blessing of instant fame in the 1970s. Such soaring popularity is usually followed by an equally steep drop. Quiche never deserved this rollercoaster ride. It's been a tradition in Alsace/Lorraine since the 16th century and shouldn't be subject to the vagaries of faddism. Besides, the quiche many Americans encountered in fern bars bore little resemblance to the true quiche— creamy custard lovingly held in a delicate pastry crust.

This section also includes recipes for vegetable dishes, meats and the treat many Americans recall as their first taste of France: French toast!

Quiche Lorraine

Quiche Lorraine

At la Madeleine quiche is one of our best-selling items. We use a puff pastry crust along with bacon and ham, which makes our quiche exceptionally flaky and so delicious.

Filling:

Preheat the oven to 375°.

Place the bacon in a medium skillet and cook until crisp. Remove the bacon from the skillet and drain on paper towels. Set aside.

Sprinkle the bacon evenly over the bottom of the baked and cooled tart shell. Top bacon with the diced ham and then the shredded Gruyère. Set aside.

Whisk the half & half, eggs, salt, pepper and nutmeg together in a medium bowl and pour the filling into the prepared tart shell. Do not overfill the tart shell or it may spill over in the oven.

Place the quiche on a baking sheet and place in the preheated oven.

Bake for 25 to 30 minutes or until the quiche is puffed and golden brown on top.

Remove the quiche from the oven and set on a wire rack to cool. Cool slightly before slicing into wedges. Quiche can be served warm or at room temperature.

Serves 8   Moderate

Tart Shell:

Preheat oven to 350°.

Set aside a 9-inch tart pan, preferably with a removable bottom.

Thaw the sheet of puff pastry for 20 to 30 minutes at room temperature. Unfold the dough and place it on a lightly floured surface. Roll the dough out until it is large enough to fit the tart pan, allowing enough dough to go up the sides. Carefully transfer the dough to the tart pan using the rolling pin. Ease the dough into the pan. Using your hands, gently press and fit the dough into place, allowing excess dough to hang over the sides of the pan. Roll the top of the pan with the rolling pin. Cut a piece of parchment paper into a 9-inch circle and place the circle on top of the dough. Cover the paper with the dried beans or pie weights. This holds the dough down and prevents it from puffing during baking. Place the pan in the oven and bake for 20 to 30 minutes, or until golden brown. Check the color by removing the pan from the oven and lifting an edge of the paper. When baked, lift the parchment with the beans or weights and pour them onto another surface to cool. Set the crust aside on a wire rack to cool before filling.

Easy

At French street fairs there are "quiche trucks."

Quiche Lorraine

3 slices smoked bacon, diced

1 prebaked 9-inch tart shell

¼ cup diced ham

¼ cup shredded Gruyère

3 cups half & half

4 eggs

½ teaspoon sea salt

¼ teaspoon freshly ground pepper

pinch of nutmeg

Tart Shell

1 sheet frozen puff pastry
(about 9 ½ inches x 9 ½ inches)

dried beans or pie weights

Alsacian Onion Tart

Tarte à l'Oignon

4 slices smoked bacon (about ¼ pound
cut into ¼-inch dice)

2 tablespoons unsalted butter

4 yellow onions, peeled and thinly sliced
(about 1 ½ pounds)

2 tablespoons flour

1 cup half & half

sea salt, to taste

freshly ground black pepper, to taste

2 eggs

1 prebaked 9-inch tart shell
(see recipe page 53)

As an apprentice baker in Alsace, Chef Remy had to do a lot of jobs that no one else wanted to do. One of the first jobs he had was to peel and slice bag after bag of onions for Tarte Alsacienne, or Onion Tart. This savory tart was made in large trays and then cut into squares and sold by the piece. Chef Remy made so many of them as an apprentice, he still remembers the recipe by heart.

Preheat the oven to 375°.

Place the diced bacon pieces in a skillet large enough to hold it in a single layer (and large enough for the onions later) and cook until crisp. Remove the bacon from the skillet and drain on paper towels. Set aside.

Pour the excess fat out of the skillet and wipe it with a paper towel. Melt the butter in the skillet over medium heat. Add the onions and cook until the onions are soft, about 20 minutes. This will seem like a lot of onions, but they will cook down. Continue cooking and stirring until the onions begin to caramelize and take on a brown color, about 10 more minutes. Add the flour and mix quickly until the flour and the onions are well combined. Reduce the heat to low, add the half & half and simmer the mixture, stirring occasionally, for 5 minutes. Season the onions with salt and pepper. Remove the skillet from the heat. Stir in the reserved bacon.

Whisk the eggs in a medium mixing bowl and combine with the onion mixture. Mix well.

Pour the filling into the baked and cooled tart shell, mounding the onions in the center.

Place the pan in the oven and bake until the filling is set and golden, about 30 to 40 minutes.

Remove from the oven and set on a wire rack to cool for 30 minutes before serving. Cut into wedges with a sharp knife.

Makes 1 9-inch tart, serves 6

Moderate

Caramelizing onions makes them sweet and delicious.

Croque Monsieur

Croque Monsieur

In France, every fête or festival has stands selling Croque Monsieurs, Quiche and Saucisson in a baguette. Croque Monsieur is street food just like hot dogs, snowcones, and sausage and pepper sandwiches in the United States.

Béchamel Sauce:

Melt the butter in a small saucepan over medium heat and then add the flour. Whisk constantly until the flour starts to brown. Gradually add the milk and simmer until the sauce is thick and smooth. Season with the salt, pepper and nutmeg.

Assembly:

Spread 1 tablespoon of the béchamel sauce on a piece of bread. Top with 1 slice of the ham and 2 tablespoons of the shredded Gruyère. Top with the second piece of bread. Spread the top of the sandwich with another layer of béchamel going all the way to the edges of the bread. Sprinkle with 2 to 3 tablespoons shredded Gruyère.

Repeat with the remaining bread.

Place the sandwiches on a baking sheet and bake for 10 to 15 minutes in a 350° oven or until the cheese is golden brown.

Serves 4

Easy

B

Béchamel Sauce

4 tablespoons unsalted butter

¼ cup all-purpose flour

1 ¼ cups milk

½ teaspoon sea salt

¼ teaspoon freshly ground pepper

pinch of nutmeg

Assembly

8 slices "Seven Grain Bread" or Brioche

4 slices ham

1 cup shredded Gruyère

Béchamel is a basic white sauce.

Savory Crêpes

1 cup all-purpose flour

3 eggs

1 ½ cups whole milk, divided use

¼ teaspoon sea salt

⅛ teaspoon ground black pepper

3 tablespoons unsalted butter, melted

Savory Crêpes

Crêpes

We've included this recipe for crêpes using all-purpose flour in case you don't want to make the more delicate buckwheat ones. Crêpes are traditionally served on Candlemas Day, February 2nd and during Carnaval. These are occasions for big parties in France and crêpes can be made quickly and easily in great quantities.

Whisk together the flour, eggs, ½ cup milk, salt and pepper in a large bowl. Continue whisking until you have a smooth batter. Add the remaining cup of milk and stir well to combine. Cover the bowl and place it in the refrigerator to chill the batter for at least 30 minutes or several hours.

Melt the butter in a small saucepan over medium heat. Just before you are ready to make the crêpes, whisk in the melted butter. The batter should be the consistency of heavy cream; if it is too thick, add milk slowly while whisking constantly until it is the right texture.

Heat a 9-inch non-stick skillet or crêpe pan over medium heat. Melt a teaspoon of butter in the pan or spray with vegetable spray and heat the pan until a drop of water "dances" across the surface.

Using a ladle or a measuring cup with a lip, pour about ¼ to ⅓ cup of the batter into the pan. Hold the pan with one hand and pour the batter in with the other. Swirl the pan while pouring so that the batter covers the pan thinly and evenly for each crêpe. Pour off any excess batter. Try not to leave any holes. After the first few crêpes you will know exactly how much batter your pan will hold.

Cook the crêpe over medium-high heat until the edges turn brown, about 15 seconds. Flip the crêpe using a small spatula and your fingers or a thin spatula. Cook on the second side for another 10 to 15 seconds. The second side will not be as evenly browned as the first side. Remove the pan from the heat and invert it over a warm plate to stack the crêpes. Keep warm until ready to use. Continue making crêpes until the batter is gone, adjusting the heat as needed.

If not using immediately, place a square of wax paper between each one; place in a resealable plastic bag and store in the refrigerator. Crêpes can be refrigerated for up to 2 days or frozen for several months. Reheat uncovered in a low oven (250°) for 15 minutes or until warm. Fill with your favorite filling.

Makes 8 (8-inch) large crêpes or 20 (6-inch) small crêpes   Easy

Stack the crêpes as you go; they will keep each other warm and soft.

Buckwheat Crêpes
Crêpes au Sarrasin

Buckwheat crêpes are dark brown and nutty tasting. These crêpes are delicate but with a little practice your crêpes can be just like the ones on the street corners in France. You can find buckwheat flour in the baking section of large grocery stores or health food markets.

Melt the 2 tablespoons butter in a small saucepan over medium heat. Leave the pan over the heat, watching all the time, until the butter turns a light caramel color and smells nutty. This is called "beurre noisette."

Sift the all-purpose and buckwheat flours together in a medium bowl, then add the salt.

In another bowl or measuring cup, whisk together the milk, eggs and melted brown butter. Add the milk mixture to the flour mixture, whisking until smooth.

Cover the bowl and place it in the refrigerator to chill for 30 minutes.

When ready to cook the crêpes, heat a 9-inch non-stick skillet or crêpe pan over medium heat. Melt a teaspoon of butter in the pan or spray with vegetable spray and then heat the pan until a drop of water "dances" across the surface.

Stir the batter. Then, using a ladle or a measuring cup with a lip, pour about ¼ to ⅓ cup of the batter into the pan. Hold the pan with one hand and pour the batter in with the other. Swirl the pan while pouring so that the batter covers the pan thinly and evenly. Pour off any excess batter. Try not to leave any holes. If there are some holes just fill them in with batter. After the first few crêpes you will know exactly how much batter your pan will hold.

Cook the crêpe over medium-high heat until the edges turn brown, about 15 seconds. Flip the crêpe using a small spatula and your fingers or a thin spatula. The crêpes are delicate so be careful not to tear them. Cook on the second side for another 10 to 15 seconds. The second side will not be as evenly browned as the first side. Remove the pan from the heat and invert it over a plate to stack the crêpes. Keep warm until ready to use. Continue making crêpes until the batter is gone, adjusting the heat as needed.

If not using immediately, place a square of waxed paper between each one; place in a resealable plastic bag and store in the refrigerator. Crêpes can be refrigerated for up to 2 days or frozen for several months. Reheat uncovered in a low oven (250°) for 15 minutes or until warm. Fill with your favorite filling.

Makes 8 (8-inch) large crêpes or 20 (6-inch) small crêpes

Easy

Ⓑ Ⓑ Ⓑ

Buckwheat Crêpes

2 tablespoons unsalted butter

¾ cup all-purpose flour

⅓ cup buckwheat flour

½ teaspoon salt

1 ½ cups milk

3 large eggs

butter for the pan or vegetable oil cooking spray, if necessary

With a non-stick pan you will be turning out crêpes like a pro.

Wild Mushroom Crêpes

4 tablespoons unsalted butter

4 cups sliced assorted wild mushrooms:
Chanterelles, Porcini, Portabello, Shitake

sea salt, to taste

freshly ground black pepper, to taste

2 tablespoons Cognac

2 tablespoons fresh herbs, minced (chervil,
tarragon, thyme, chives, parsley)

4 large or 8 small crêpes (see page 58)

1 cup beurre blanc

additional herbs for garnish

Beurre Blanc

2 tablespoons minced shallots

½ cup white wine

¼ cup champagne vinegar

1 tablespoon heavy cream

1 ¼ cups unsalted butter, chilled and cut
into ½-inch slices

½ teaspoon sea salt, or to taste

freshly ground pepper, to taste

Wild Mushroom Crêpes

Crêpes Forestières

Use any combination of mushrooms that you like in this recipe. If you can't find fresh wild mushrooms, try dried ones. Reconstitute in water according to the package directions. For added flavor substitute Cognac for some of the water.

Melt the butter in a large saucepan over medium heat. Add the sliced mushrooms and the salt and pepper. Shake the pan and toss the mushrooms to coat with butter. Cook, stirring and shaking the pan occasionally for about 10 minutes or until the mushrooms begin to give off their juices. Add the Cognac and cook until the mushrooms are tender, about 5 more minutes. Stir in the fresh herbs and remove from the heat.

To use as a filling for crêpes, warm the mushrooms. Place a crêpe, brown side down, on a serving plate. Place about ¼ to ½ cup of the mushroom mixture slightly to the side and roll the crêpe so that the filling is enclosed. Garnish with Beurre Blanc sauce and freshly chopped herbs.

Beurre Blanc:

Place the shallots, wine and vinegar in a heavy nonreactive saucepan. Place the pan over medium-high heat and bring to a boil. Continue boiling the mixture to reduce it to approximately 3 tablespoons of liquid, stirring as necessary. Remove the pan from the heat. Whisk the cream into the liquid. Reduce the heat to low and place the pan back on the heat. Whisk 3 pieces of butter into the reduced liquid. The butter should not completely melt but instead become creamy. Add the remaining pieces of butter slowly, whisking constantly. Do not add more butter until each piece is absorbed. Do not allow the butter to melt completely or the sauce will not be bound together. Remove the pan from the heat as necessary, if the sauce becomes too hot. This process should just take 2 to 3 minutes. When all the butter is incorporated, remove the sauce from the heat. The sauce should be as thick as heavy cream, smooth and emulsified. Whisk again. Taste the sauce and season with salt and pepper to taste. Serve at once or pour into a Thermos to keep warm for a short period of time.

Serves 4   Moderate

These mushrooms make a delicious topping for a juicy steak.

Shrimp Crêpes

Crêpes aux Crevettes

Serve these crêpes for a Mother's Day brunch or as a first course at a formal dinner. The crêpes and the filling can be made ahead of time, but fill the crêpes when you are ready to serve so they are at their best.

Place the olive oil in a medium sauté pan over medium heat. Add the garlic and cook until it is fragrant and turns translucent, about 4 minutes. Add the shrimp and cook, stirring and shaking the pan for an additional 6 minutes, or until the shrimp turn opaque and pink.

Remove the pan from the heat and add the Cognac while shaking the skillet. Return the pan to the heat, holding it carefully away from direct heat or flame as the Cognac may catch fire. Cook, shaking constantly, for about 3 minutes or until the Cognac evaporates and the pan begins to sizzle. Add the cream and cook, stirring frequently, until the sauce has reduced by about one-third, about 4 to 5 minutes. Remove from the heat and stir in the butter and tarragon. Season to taste with salt and pepper.

Place a crêpe, brown side down, on a serving plate. Place about ¼ to ½ cup of the shrimp mixture slightly to the side and roll the crêpe so that the filling is enclosed. Serve immediately.

Serves 4   Moderate

Ham & Gruyère Crêpes

Crêpes au Jambon et Gruyère

Make savory or buckwheat crêpes according to the preceding recipes. As soon as you flip the crêpe over to cook the second side, sprinkle ⅛ cup of the Gruyère on one-half of the crêpe. Top with ½ ounce of the ham. Fold the side of the crêpe over, enclosing the ham and cheese. As the cheese melts, flip the crêpe over one more time. Slide the crêpe onto a serving plate and fold in quarters. Serve immediately while the crêpes are still warm.

Serves 4   Easy

Shrimp Crêpes

2 tablespoons extra virgin olive oil

1 garlic clove, minced

1 pound large shrimp, peeled and deveined

3 tablespoons Cognac

½ cup heavy cream

2 tablespoons unsalted butter

2 tablespoons minced fresh tarragon

sea salt, to taste

ground black pepper, to taste

4 large or 8 small crêpes (see recipe page 58)

Ham & Gruyère Crêpese

8 (8-inch) crêpes

1 cup shredded Gruyère

4 ounces good-quality ham, sliced

Crêpes can be frozen for up to a month.

Ratatouille Crêpes

Crêpes à la Ratatouille

Ratatouille is a traditional dish of Provence, where these summer vegetables are a mainstay. There are two ways to make ratatouille: either simmer all the vegetables together for a few hours until they form a thick sauce or cook them separately. We like to cook the vegetables separately so that the flavors and colors of the vegetables stay crisp and distinct.

Preheat the oven to 400°.

Put the eggplant cubes into a colander and add 1 tablespoon salt. Stir and let sit for 1 hour. Rinse the eggplant and pat dry. Put the eggplant into a baking pan with 2 tablespoons olive oil. Stir and bake for 25 to 30 minutes, or until soft.

Meanwhile, heat 1 tablespoon olive oil until fragrant. Add the onions, cover and cook over medium heat until the onions are golden brown, about 20 to 25 minutes. Remove from the pan and season with salt and pepper.

Heat another tablespoon of olive oil and add the peppers. Cover and cook over medium heat until soft, about 15 minutes. Stir occasionally. Add to the reserved onions.

Heat another tablespoon of olive oil and add the zucchini. Cover and cook over medium heat until tender, about 15 minutes. Add to the onions and peppers.

Heat the remaining oil and add the tomatoes, garlic and the Herbes de Provence. Cover and cook over medium heat until soft, about 15 minutes. Add the vermouth and stir. Add the tomatoes to the other vegetables.

When the eggplant is cooked, add it to the other vegetables. If using right away, place mixture back in the saucepan and heat thoroughly.

To use as a filling for crêpes, warm the ratatouille. Place a crêpe, brown side down, on a serving plate. Place about ¼ to ½ cup of the ratatouille mixture slightly to the side and roll the crêpe so that the filling is enclosed. Serve immediately.

Moderate
Serves 4

B

Ratatouille Crêpes

1 small eggplant, cut into 1-inch cubes

1 tablespoon sea salt

6 tablespoons olive oil, divided use

3 yellow onions, peeled and sliced

sea salt, to taste

freshly ground black pepper, to taste

1 large green pepper, cored, seeded and cut into 1-inch pieces

1 large red pepper, cored, seeded and cut into 1-inch pieces

1 zucchini, cut into 1-inch cubes

1 pound tomatoes, diced

2 cloves garlic, peeled and minced

1 teaspoon Herbes de Provence

¼ cup dry vermouth or white wine

4 large or 8 small crêpes
(see recipe page 58)

Ratatouille tastes even better the next day.

63

1 cup all-purpose flour

pinch of salt

2 teaspoons granulated sugar

1 tablespoon canola oil

2 teaspoons rum

2 eggs

1 ¼ cups milk

unsalted butter as needed for pan

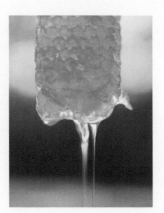

Sweet Crêpes

Crêpes Sucrées

The variations for sweet crêpes are endless: Nutella and banana, maple syrup and butter, fruit preserves, honey and walnuts, whipped cream or fresh fruit to name a few. Another classic option: serve stacks of warm crêpes with a bowl of sugar and a bowl of fresh-squeezed lemon juice and let your guests serve themselves.

Whisk together the flour, salt, sugar, canola oil, rum and eggs in a large bowl. Pour the milk in slowly, whisking constantly until you have a smooth batter.

Cover the bowl and place it in the refrigerator to chill the batter for at least 30 minutes or several hours.

When you are ready to make the crêpes, remove from the refrigerator and stir. The batter should be the consistency of heavy cream. If it is too thick, add milk slowly while whisking constantly until it is the right texture.

Heat a 9-inch non-stick skillet or crêpe pan over medium heat. Melt a teaspoon of butter in the pan or spray with vegetable spray and heat the pan until a drop of water "dances" across the surface.

Using a ladle or a measuring cup with a lip, pour about ¼ to ⅓ cup of the batter into the pan. Hold the pan with one hand and pour the batter in with the other. Swirl the pan while pouring so that the batter covers the pan thinly and evenly for each crêpe. Pour off any excess batter. Try not to leave any holes. After the first few crêpes you will know exactly how much batter your pan will hold.

Cook the crêpe over medium-high heat until the edges turn brown, about 15 seconds. Flip the crêpe using a small spatula and your fingers or a thin spatula. Cook on the second side for another 10 to 15 seconds. The second side will not be as evenly browned as the first side. Remove the pan from the heat and invert it over a warm plate to stack the crêpes. Keep warm until ready to use. Continue making crêpes until the batter is gone, adjusting the heat as needed.

Fill with your favorite filling.

Makes 8 (8-inch) large crêpes or 20 (6-inch) small crêpes

Easy

As kids we grew up on Nutella, the European answer to peanut butter.

Waffles

Gaufres

Waffles or "gaufres" are sold on the street corners or at festivals just like crêpes in France. This recipe can be used for thick Belgian waffles or thin crisp ones. Waffles are very versatile; you can eat them for breakfast with butter and maple syrup, for brunch or a light supper topped with creamed chicken. For a fabulous dessert, top with banana ice cream, sliced bananas and chocolate syrup.

Waffles

12 tablespoons unsalted butter

2 ¼ cups all-purpose flour

2 tablespoons granulated sugar

2 tablespoons baking powder

1 teaspoon baking soda

1 teaspoon salt

1 teaspoon natural vanilla extract

1 ½ cups milk

3 eggs

Melt the 12 tablespoons butter in a small saucepan over medium heat. Leave the pan over the heat, watching all the time, until the butter turns a light caramel color and smells nutty. Dip the bottom of the pan in cold water as soon as the butter reaches the right color to stop the cooking process. Butter cooked this way is called "beurre noisette."

Whisk to combine the flour, sugar, baking powder, baking soda and salt in a large bowl.

Mix the vanilla and the milk together and whisk into the flour mixture. Add the "beurre noisette" and whisk until well blended.

Add the eggs, one at a time, mixing well after each addition.

When ready to cook, preheat the waffle iron according to manufacturer's directions. Spray the waffle iron with a vegetable oil cooking spray.

If the batter is too thick, stir in some milk to lighten it.

When the waffle iron is ready, pour about ½ to ¾ cup of batter into the iron, covering most of the grids. The amount of batter will vary depending on the size of the waffle iron. Cook for 3 minutes or until golden brown.

Check waffle by barely lifting the top. It will not stick when cooked. If more browning is needed, just close the top and continue cooking for another minute or so. Remove the waffles with a fork and set on a baking sheet. Keep the cooked waffles, in a single layer, in a warm (200°) oven. Continue cooking the waffles until the batter is finished.

Serve with maple syrup and butter or whipped cream and fruit if desired.

Makes 8 (7-inch) waffles

Easy

Don't be alarmed if your first waffle isn't perfect — the second one will be!

French Toast Royale

Ⓑ

French Toast Royale

4 eggs

¾ cup milk

2 tablespoons granulated sugar

½ teaspoon natural vanilla extract

8 slices Muesli bread, sliced ¾-inch thick

1 tablespoon unsalted butter

½ cup sliced bananas

½ cup sliced strawberries

2 teaspoons granulated sugar

confectioners' sugar for garnish

maple or boysenberry syrup, optional

French Toast was originally developed on the farm as a way to use up stale bread. At la Madeleine, we use our Muesli bread and cut it into thick slices so that the toast is moist but not soggy. Our Muesli bread, studded with raisins and nuts, adds great texture and flavor to our French toast making it "royale."

Whisk the eggs, milk, sugar and vanilla together in a large bowl.

Pour the batter into a 13 x 9-inch pan. Lay the bread slices in the batter in a single layer. Let them soak for 2 minutes, then turn them over and let them soak for 5 more minutes, or until all of the batter is absorbed.

Melt the butter over medium heat in a non-stick sauté pan large enough to hold 3 or 4 pieces of bread at a time. Carefully transfer several bread slices to the sauté pan using a spatula to lift the bread. Arrange the slices in the pan. You will probably have to prepare several batches. Cook the bread for 2 to 3 minutes on one side or until golden brown. Flip the bread and cook for another 2 minutes. Turn again if necessary for additional browning. Set cooked toast on a baking sheet in a single layer and place in a warm (200°) oven to keep warm.

While the bread is cooking, combine the bananas and strawberries in a bowl and sprinkle with the sugar. Toss lightly and let sit until ready to serve.

At serving time, place 1 slice of the cooked French toast on each of 4 serving plates. Divide the fruit and place equal portions on top of the French toast. Top each with a second slice and dust with confectioners' sugar. Serve immediately. Top with maple or boysenberry syrup if desired.

Serves 4

Easy

Substitute raisin bread or brioche for the Muesli bread if you like.

Diplomat

1 ¼ cups milk

6 eggs

1 teaspoon natural vanilla extract

½ cup granulated sugar

4 croissants (about 8 cups cubed)

½ cup golden raisins

1 cup whipped heavy cream, optional

mint leaves for garnish, optional

Raspberry Coulis

1 pint fresh raspberries

¼ cup granulated sugar

Diplomat

Diplomate

The Diplomat is another la Madeleine favorite. We serve this rich version of bread pudding for breakfast, brunch and also for dessert throughout the day. This popular dessert is found in local boulangeries all over France.

Diplomat:

Preheat the oven to 400°.

Butter the insides of 4 6 – or 8 – ounce ramekins or custard cups. Set aside.

Whisk the milk, eggs, vanilla and sugar together in a large bowl. Slice the croissants (day-old ones will be easier to slice) into 1-inch pieces and add to the milk mixture. Stir in the raisins and set aside to let the croissants soak for 30 minutes. The croissants will absorb most of the liquid during this time.

Divide the croissant-custard mixture among the buttered ramekins. Mound the mixture above the top of the ramekins if necessary.

Place the ramekins into a 13 x 9 x 2-inch baking pan. Create a water bath by adding ½-inch boiling water to the pan.

Place the pan into the oven and reduce the temperature to 350°. Bake the ramekins for 30 minutes or until a knife inserted in the middle comes out moist but clean. The custards will be puffed and golden brown on top. Remove the ramekins from the water bath and let cool slightly.

At serving time, run a sharp knife around the edges of each of the ramekins and unmold the diplomats. Set each one on a plate right side up and surround it with about ¼ cup Raspberry Coulis. Serve with freshly whipped cream topped with a mint leaf if desired.

Raspberry Coulis:

Rinse the raspberries and place in the container of a blender. Add the sugar. Blend on high speed until the raspberries are liquefied and the sugar is dissolved, about 3 minutes. Remove the Coulis and serve at once or place in an airtight container in the refrigerator.

Serves 4

Easy

 Decorate plates in a snap by putting the Coulis in a squeeze bottle and drizzling.

Apple Potato Gratin

Gratin Dauphinois aux Pommes

La Madeleine sends a group of bakery managers to France every year to learn about French food, the culture and traditions. This version of the classic Dauphinois was inspired by their recent trip to Normandy where apples play a big role in the local cuisine. The apples and bacon add a sweet and smoky note to the lush potatoes.

❧

Preheat the oven to 425°.

Place the diced bacon and the sliced onions in a medium skillet. Cook over medium heat until the bacon is cooked but not crisp and the onions are soft and translucent. This should take about 10 minutes. Set aside.

Combine the cream, half & half, garlic and the salt and pepper in a large saucepan. Add the sliced potatoes and apple slices and stir well to combine. Bring to a simmer over medium heat and cook, stirring occasionally with a wooden spoon, for 25 minutes or until the potatoes are tender. Do not let the potatoes boil.

Add the bacon and onion mixture to the potatoes and adjust the seasonings. Place the potatoes into a buttered 8 x 10-inch baking dish. Sprinkle the top of the mixture with the Gruyère.

Put the pan on a baking sheet to catch any spills and place in the oven. Bake for 20 minutes on the center rack or until the top of the gratin is crusty and golden brown.

Serves 6

Moderate

Apple Potato Gratin

6 slices bacon, diced

1 medium yellow onion, sliced

2 cups heavy cream

1 cup half & half

1 clove garlic, minced

2 teaspoons sea salt

ground black pepper, to taste

2 pounds red potatoes, sliced

2 Red Delicious apples, peeled, cored and thinly sliced

1 ½ cups shredded Gruyère

A gratin can be made a few hours ahead and reheated just before serving.

Potato Cakes with Boursin

2 russet potatoes (about 1 pound) peeled and grated

¾ teaspoon sea salt

½ teaspoon freshly ground black pepper

4 ounces Boursin (about ½ cup)

4 teaspoons finely chopped chives

2 tablespoons olive oil

additional chives for garnish

Potato Cakes with Boursin

Galettes de Pommes de Terre au Boursin

We get a lot of requests for our Potato Galette recipe; this isn't quite the same recipe, but it is a tasty variation. Be sure to use Boursin in this recipe since the other herb cheeses don't have the robust flavor needed to accent the potatoes. Russet potatoes are the best choice; you need the starch to hold the galettes together.

Grate the potatoes by hand or with a food processor. The grated potatoes should measure about 3 ½ cups. Place the grated potatoes in a dry tea towel and squeeze to remove as much water as possible.

Place the potatoes, without rinsing, in a large bowl and add the salt and pepper. Mix together with a fork to evenly distribute the salt and pepper.

Divide the Boursin into 4 pieces and flatten slightly into a circle about 2 ½ to 3 inches across. Sprinkle the chives evenly over the Boursin. Set aside.

Heat the olive oil in a large sauté pan over medium heat until fragrant.

Using a ⅓-cup measure, scoop 1 measure of grated potatoes and place in the pan. Flatten with a spatula to form a 4-inch circle. Repeat 3 more times, making 4 cakes. Place the Boursin circles on each of the cakes.

Scoop another ⅓ cup of grated potatoes and place on top of the cheese on each cake. Press down with a spatula, enclosing the cheese and the chives.

Cook until the bottoms are golden, about 6 minutes. Turn the cakes over and cook for another 5 to 6 minutes or until the bottoms are golden.

Garnish with additional chives if desired. Serve immediately while still warm.

Makes 4 cakes

Moderate

Don't grate the potatoes ahead of time; they will turn brown.

Roasted Asparagus with Lemon Oil

Asperges Rôti à l'Huile de Citron

In France, asparagus is grown under mounds of earth to keep the stalks white and delicate. Here, you can usually only find white asparagus in a can, which is not at all the same. In America, the green stalks of asparagus and rosy new potatoes signal the first vegetables of spring.

Preheat the oven to 500°.

If the asparagus are thin (about the size of a pencil), snap the woody ends off at the natural break. If they are thick, snap off the woody ends and peel with a vegetable peeler.

Whisk together the olive oil, lemon zest, lemon juice, salt and pepper in a small bowl.

Lay the asparagus into a shallow 8 x 8-inch baking pan. Make sure all the asparagus are facing in the same direction. Pour the olive oil and lemon mixture over the asparagus and shake the pan so that all the asparagus are coated with the oil.

Place the pan in the oven and roast for 10 minutes, shaking the pan every 2 to 3 minutes or until the asparagus are tender and lightly browned.

Serves 4

Easy

Roasted Asparagus with Lemon Oil

2 pounds fresh asparagus

3 tablespoons extra virgin olive oil

1 teaspoon lemon zest

juice of 1 organic lemon

sea salt, to taste

freshly ground black pepper, to taste

Sweet, young asparagus cooks very quickly.

Tomato Provençal

Tomates à la Provençale

Whole tomatoes give any dish a quick boost of color and flavor. Herbes de Provence is a blend of basil, fennel seed, lavender, marjoram, rosemary, sage and thyme. Basil or oregano is a good substitute, but garlic is essential to any Provençal dish. Only use ripe, preferably vine-ripened tomatoes, or you will be disappointed in the texture and taste.

Preheat the oven to 350°.

Using a sharp knife, core the tomato, removing the stem end and going about 1 inch into the tomato. If the tomato wobbles, cut a small slice from the bottom. Salt and pepper the inside of the tomato. Drizzle the inside of each tomato with a teaspoon of the olive oil. Sprinkle the garlic, herbs and then the bread crumbs evenly over the oil. Sprinkle with the chopped parsley and then top with the Parmesan.

Place the tomatoes into individual ramekins or into a baking dish large enough to hold the tomatoes without touching.

Place the baking pan into the oven and bake for 15 minutes or until the tops are golden brown and the tomatoes are soft.

Serve immediately while still warm.

Serves 4

Easy

Tomato Provençal

4 medium-sized ripe tomatoes

sea salt, to taste

freshly ground black pepper, to taste

1 ½ tablespoons extra virgin olive oil

1 clove garlic, minced

1 teaspoon Herbes de Provence

½ cup fresh bread crumbs

2 teaspoons finely chopped parsley

2 teaspoons grated Parmesan

You can fill the tomatoes ahead of time and bake just before serving.

Breakfast Sausage

Saucisse

You will be amazed at how easy it is to make your own sausage. Have the butcher grind the pork in one-third fat to to two-thirds meat proportion. Be sure to keep the ground pork cold so that the texture stays coarse.

Then season the ground pork to your liking. To test for seasoning, cook a small amount. Don't taste the raw pork mixture.

Thoroughly mix all the ingredients in a large bowl.

To make patties, simply shape in your hand and pat into a small flat disc.

Place the patties in a large sauté pan and cook over high heat for 2 to 3 minutes or until brown and crusty but not burnt. Turn the patties over and brown the other side. Lower the heat to medium-low and cook until the patties are cooked through, about 8 to 10 minutes. Drain on paper towels.

Serve immediately while still warm.

Serves 6

Easy

Breakfast Sausage

2 pounds pork butt, coarsely ground

2 teaspoons freshly ground black pepper, or to taste

1 ½ teaspoons sea salt, or to taste

2 teaspoons sage, ground

1 teaspoon thyme, dried

Adding anise seed will give your sausage a taste of **Provence**.

Pepper Bacon

1 pound sliced lean bacon

2 teaspoons freshly ground pepper, or to taste

Caramelized Bacon

1 pound sliced lean bacon

1 ½ cups brown sugar

Salmon Bacon

2 teaspoons extra virgin olive oil

8 ounces smoked salmon, thinly sliced

juice of one organic lemon

freshly ground black pepper, to taste

Pepper Bacon

Bacon au Poivre

You can now buy peppered and other flavored bacons in the grocery store, but if you want to make your own it is very easy to do. You can also microwave the bacon if you prefer. Plan on 1 minute per slice.

Preheat the oven to 400°.

Arrange the bacon on a baking sheet with sides and sprinkle evenly with the pepper. Bake for 25 minutes, or until the bacon is crisp. Reverse the pan halfway through the baking time so that the bacon cooks evenly. Drain on paper towels and keep warm until ready to serve.

Serves 6 Easy

Caramelized Bacon

Bacon Caramelisé

Preheat the oven to 350°.

Place the brown sugar into a shallow dish, then roll the bacon slices in the sugar until both sides are well coated. Place the bacon on a broiler pan and bake until golden brown, about 15 to 18 minutes. Turn the bacon over halfway through the cooking time, using tongs. Cool the bacon on a rack. Since the bacon gets crisper as it cools, serve at room temperature.

Serves 6 Easy

Salmon Bacon

Bacon de Saumon

Heat the oil in a medium sauté pan over medium heat until fragrant. Add the salmon and cook until the salmon is lightly browned, about 4 minutes. Turn the salmon over and cook until lightly browned. Add the lemon juice and season with fresh pepper.

Serves 2 Easy

Bacon tends to disappear, so make sure you have plenty.

Les Notes

Les Pains et Pâtisseries

Breads & Pastries

Muesli Bread
Kugelhopf
Kugelhopf with Bacon and Onions
Orange Brioche
Ardennaise Cake
Crème Fraîche Coffee Cake
Almond Cake
Lemon and Ginger Cake
Walnut and Dried Apricot Cake
Almond Cookies
Cranberry Pecan Scones
Blueberry Muffins
Doughnuts
Croissant Dough
Chocolate Croissant
Pain Raisin
Pretzel Croissants
Croissants
Cherry Custard

The recipes included here fall into two categories: breads and pastries, or in French, les viennoiseries et les pâtisseries. In America, we tend to lump the two together under the heading of "baked goods." The French do not. In fact, if you wander into a French bakery or boulangerie, you're likely to find only breads, rolls, croissants and other yeast-risen items. You'll have to go to the pâtisserie for éclairs, tartes, napoléons, meringues and the like.

It seems like a nitpicky distinction until you understand the seriousness with which the French view baking. You see, in France, baking is like raising a child. This analogy holds true for a number of reasons:

1) Both are treated as undertakings of great importance.

2) Everyone who's done either has his or her own idea of how it is best accomplished.

3) Both are likely to mess up your house.

4) Both are challenging and gratifying; quintessential labors of love.

The result of the French obsession with baking is a reputation for the world's greatest breads and pastries. But don't let that intimidate you. You'll find that if you follow our recipes, your results will be worthy of their authors, our own la Madeleine bakers. It helps to keep in mind that baking is a matter of kitchen chemistry. Unlike other types of cooking that invite improvisation, accuracy in measuring and following directions is critical to the baker's success.

Now, go forth and bake, taking comfort in the knowledge that the challenges (unlike those of child-rearing) are easily overcome.

Muesli Bread

Pain au Muesli

Making your own bread can seem a little intimidating, but our bakers have some tricks to make bread baking easier.

Yeast rises best at room temperature, around 70° to 75°. A draft-free location ensures that the dough will rise evenly and covering the dough with a tea towel or plastic wrap keeps a skin from forming. To save time, mix up your dough the night before and let it rise in the refrigerator overnight. The cold will slow down the yeast and allow the flavor of the bread to develop more fully. Your dough has risen if it does not spring back when you press it with your finger.

Mix the all-purpose flour, whole-wheat flour, muesli and salt together in the bowl of an electric mixer fitted with the dough hook.

Add the yeast, honey and canola oil. Add just enough milk to form a soft dough and mix at medium speed until the dough is smooth and forms a ball around the hook, about 10 minutes. Check the machine from time to time to make sure it does not "walk" during the kneading. Scrape the bowl if necessary with a spatula.

Place the dough into an oiled bowl and cover with a tea towel. Set aside to rise at room temperature in a draft-free location until almost doubled in volume, about 2 hours.

Divide the dough in half and shape each half into a circle. Cut each half with a sharp knife, about ½ inch deep, into 8 wedges. Do not cut all the way through, just enough that the bread will open like a flower during baking.

Place each loaf into a 9-inch round baking pan, cover with a tea towel and let the loaves rise again at room temperature until the dough reaches the top of the pan, about 2 hours.

Preheat the oven to 400°.

Dust the tops of the loaves with whole-wheat flour. Place the loaves in the oven and bake for 25 to 30 minutes or until golden brown on top.

Let cool on a wire rack.

See the illustrations in the glossary for further instructions on folding and shaping dough.

Makes 2 loaves Moderate

Muesli Bread

3 ½ cups all-purpose flour

¾ cup whole-wheat flour

1 cup unsweetened muesli flakes

2 teaspoons salt

1 package (¼ ounce) dry fast-rising yeast

2 tablespoons honey

2 tablespoons canola oil

1 ¾ cups to 2 cups milk

Use prepared dry Muesli, not fresh, for this recipe.

½ cup dark raisins

2 tablespoons Kirsch liquor

2 tablespoons water

Dough

4 cups bread flour

½ cup granulated sugar

1 teaspoon salt

1 package (¼ ounce) dry fast-rising yeast

3 eggs

1 cup warm milk (100°)

8 tablespoons unsalted butter, softened

2 tablespoons butter, melted for the mold

18 whole almonds with the peel on, one for the bottom of each runnel of the mold

2 tablespoons confectioners' sugar

Kugelhopf

Kugelhopf

Every year in June, the town of Ribeauville holds a Fête du Kugelhopf. This fête is held in honor of the Magi who, according to the local folklore, walked from Bethlehem to Cologne where they were treated hospitably by a baker named Kugel. To show their thanks, they baked a cake in a turban shape and named it after the baker Kugel. Our Chef Remy did his apprenticeship in a bakery in Ribeauville where the fête originated. He baked countless Kugelhopfs as an apprentice and shares his mother's recipe.

Needs some overnight preparation.

Raisins:

Combine the raisins, Kirsch and water in a small bowl. Cover and let macerate overnight.

Dough:

The total preparation and baking time for the bread is about 5 to 6 hours, so it would be best to begin the dough in the morning.

Combine the flour, sugar and salt in the bowl of an electric mixer fitted with the dough hook attachment. Mix briefly at low speed, about 1 minute, to blend. Add the yeast and eggs and mix at low speed. Immediately add the milk slowly, adding only enough to make the dough combine. Scrape the sides of the bowl as needed.

Mix at low speed for 5 minutes.

When the dough is well combined, increase the speed to medium and knead for 15 minutes. Check the machine from time to time to make sure it does not "walk" during the kneading. Scrape the bowl if necessary with a spatula. The dough should begin to pull away from the sides of the bowl and be smooth and soft.

Add the softened butter, about 2 tablespoons at a time, and continue mixing at low speed until the dough is smooth and forms a ball around the hook, about 5 minutes. Occasionally stop the mixer and scrape down the bowl with a dough scraper to help mix the butter. Add the raisins and mix briefly until well combined.

Ribeauville is near the border of France and Germany.

Kugelhopf (suite)

Cover the bowl with plastic wrap and set aside to let rise at room temperature in a draft-free location until almost doubled in volume, about 3 hours.

In the meantime, melt the remaining butter and, using a pastry brush, butter the entire inside of a 9-inch Kugelhopf mold. Line the bottom of the mold with the whole almonds. Place an almond in each of the runnels, or indentations, on the diagonal with the point of the almond facing toward the center of the mold. Brush the almonds lightly with water. This will keep the almonds stuck to the dough.

Once the dough has doubled in volume, use a dough scraper to remove the dough from the mixing bowl and turn onto a lightly floured flat surface. Lightly sprinkle the dough with flour and gently knead the dough to form another ball. If the dough sticks, you may dust it with more flour. Don't use too much flour. This will be a soft dough and a tiny bit sticky.

Make a hole with your finger in the center of the dough and then place the dough in the buttered Kugelhopf mold around the center spike.

Let rise at room temperature for another 1 to 2 hours or until the dough is 1 ½ times its original size. The dough should not exceed the top of the pan by more than 1 inch.

Preheat the oven to 325° about 15 minutes before baking.

Place the pan in the oven and bake the Kugelhopf for 35 minutes or until the bread is golden brown.

Immediately invert on a rack to cool, almond side up.

Dust with confectioners' sugar before serving.

Makes 1 large Kugelhopf

Moderate

Serve for breakfast, brunch or even as an apéritif.

Kugelhopf with Bacon & Walnuts

Kugelhopf au Bacon et aux Noix

This bread is perfect for breakfast, on its own, or served with a salad for a light lunch. Enjoy it even more as an accompaniment to a glass of Riesling before dinner. Chef Fernand likes to slice this bread and make sandwiches, then stack the sandwiches back up as a Pain Surprise.

Sauté the diced bacon in a small skillet over low heat. Do not let the bacon brown. Using a slotted spoon, remove the bacon from the pan and let it drain on a paper towel. Sauté the chopped onions in the bacon fat over low heat until the onions are tender and translucent, about 5 minutes. Mix the bacon and the onion together. Set aside.

In the bowl of an electric mixer fitted with the dough hook attachment, combine the flour, yeast, sugar and salt. Add the beaten eggs. With the machine running at low speed, add enough milk to form a soft and sticky dough. When the dough is well combined increase the speed to medium and knead for 15 minutes. Check the machine from time to time to make sure it does not "walk" during the kneading. Scrape the bowl if necessary with a spatula. The dough should begin to pull away from the sides of the bowl and be smooth and soft.

Add the softened butter, about 2 tablespoons at a time, and continue mixing at low speed until the dough is smooth and forms a ball around the hook, about 5 minutes. Occasionally stop the mixer and scrape down the bowl with a dough scraper to help mix the butter. Add the reserved bacon and onion mixture, the chopped walnuts and thyme.

Cover the bowl with plastic wrap and set aside to let rise at room temperature in a draft-free location until it has almost doubled in volume, about 1 ½ hours.

In the meantime, melt the remaining butter and, using a pastry brush, butter the entire inside of a 9-inch Kugelhopf mold. Line the bottom of the mold with the whole walnuts. Place a walnut in each of the runnels or indentations. Brush the walnuts lightly with water. This will keep the walnuts stuck to the dough.

Kugelhopf with Bacon & Walnuts

¼ pound finely diced bacon

1 small onion, finely chopped

4 cups bread flour

1 package (¼ ounce) dry fast-rising yeast

1 tablespoon granulated sugar

1 teaspoon salt

3 eggs, beaten

1 scant cup whole milk

10 tablespoons unsalted butter, softened

12 walnut halves or enough for each runnel

¼ cup chopped walnuts

1 ½ teaspoons dried thyme

Kugelhopf with Bacon & Walnuts (suite)

Kugelhopf au Bacon et aux Noix

Once the dough has doubled in volume, use a dough scraper to remove the dough from the mixing bowl and turn onto a lightly floured flat surface. Lightly sprinkle the dough with flour and gently knead the dough to form a ball. If the dough sticks, you may dust it with more flour. Don't use too much flour. This will be a soft dough and a tiny bit sticky.

Make a hole with your finger in the center of the dough and then place the dough in the buttered Kugelhopf mold around the center spike. Cover the dough lightly with a tea towel.

Let the dough rise at room temperature for another hour or until the dough is 1 ½ times its original size. The dough should not exceed the top of the pan by more than 1 inch.

Preheat the oven to 350° about 15 minutes before baking.

Place the pan in the oven and bake the Kugelhopf for 40 to 45 minutes or until the bread is golden brown and sounds hollow when tapped.

Immediately invert on a rack to cool, walnut side up.

Moderate

Makes 1 large Kugelhopf

Kugelhopf molds are made in the town of Soufflenheim.

Orange Brioche
Brioche Landaise

This delicately flavored bread is traditionally made on Saturday and served after Sunday Mass. The extra day gives the flavors time to develop. You can find orange flower water, a product of Southern France, in specialty food stores. Increase the rum and vanilla to 3 teaspoons if you have trouble finding orange flower water. This bread is made using a sponge or "levain" starter to make it rise.

The total preparation and baking time for this bread is about 8 hours, so it would be best to begin the dough in the morning.

Levain:

Dissolve the yeast in the warm milk in the bowl of an electric mixer fitted with the paddle attachment. Add 2 cups of flour and the salt. Mix well. Add 2 eggs and mix well to combine. Cover the bowl with plastic wrap and set aside to let rise at room temperature in a draft-free location for 1 to 2 hours or until doubled in bulk.

Dough:

When the levain has risen, beat 4 eggs in the bowl of an electric mixer fitted with the paddle attachment. Add the sugar, 2 cups of flour, melted butter, vanilla, rum and orange flower water. Mix at low speed to combine. When the mixture is blended, change to the dough hook attachment and add the levain. Mix using the dough hook, at medium speed, until the dough is smooth and not sticky, about 10 to 15 minutes. If dough is still sticky, add a little more flour.

Butter a 9-inch brioche pan or non-stick baking pan with high sides. Place the dough in the pan and let rise at room temperature in a draft-free location until the dough reaches the rim of the pan, about 6 hours.

When the dough is ready to bake, beat the remaining egg with a fork and a pinch of salt. Brush the beaten egg on the top of the dough and sprinkle with the optional rock sugar crystals.

Preheat the oven to 350°. Place the pan in the oven and bake for 30 to 40 minutes or until golden brown on top.

Place on a wire rack to cool.

Makes 1 large or 2 smaller loaves

Moderate

Ⓟ
Ⓟ
Ⓟ

Levain

2 packages (¼ ounce) dry fast-rising yeast

1 cup warm milk (100°)

4 cups all-purpose flour, divided use

¼ teaspoon salt

7 eggs, divided use

Dough

1 cup granulated sugar

16 tablespoons unsalted butter, melted

2 teaspoons natural vanilla extract

2 teaspoons rum

2 teaspoons orange flower water

¼ cup rock sugar crystals, optional

Serve this bread with unsalted butter and orange marmalade.

Ardennaise Cake

Brioche Ardennaise

ⓟ

ⓟ

ⓟ

Brioche

2 tablespoons lukewarm water

1 package (¼ ounce) dry
fast-rising yeast

4 cups bread flour

1 cup milk

1 ½ teaspoons salt

2 large eggs

¼ cup plus 3 tablespoons
granulated sugar

1 teaspoon natural vanilla extract

8 tablespoons unsalted butter, softened

Brioche dough is the base for many French pastries and desserts. This dough can be a little tricky to work with because of the high ratio of butter to flour, but this particular recipe is fairly foolproof. We recommend using bread flour since it has a higher gluten level, which provides a web for the yeast, helping it rise. Chilling the dough overnight makes the dough softer and more pliable. The brioche in this recipe can be baked as bread in a brioche pan with the traditional knot or in any recipe calling for Brioche.

Requires overnight preparation.

Brioche:

Mix the lukewarm (100°) water with yeast and set aside for 10 minutes. The yeast will begin to proof, expand and become foamy. Using an electric mixer fitted with the dough hook attachment, combine the flour, milk, yeast mixture, salt, eggs, ¼ cup granulated sugar and vanilla. Mix at low speed until the dough is well combined, about 3 minutes. Increase the speed to medium and mix until the dough is smooth and detaches from the side of the bowl, about 15 minutes. The dough should form a ball around the dough hook. The dough will be soft and pliable and a bit sticky.

In a separate small bowl, combine the butter and the remaining 3 tablespoons of sugar. Blend with a spoon until the mixture is smooth. Slowly add the butter mixture to the dough, about 2 tablespoons at a time, while the machine is running. Mix until the butter is completely incorporated and the dough is smooth and elastic, but not sticky. Lightly flour a bowl that will accommodate the dough. Form the dough into a ball, place it in the bowl and refrigerate 6 to 8 hours or overnight.

The next day, divide the brioche dough into 8 balls about 4 ounces each for individual brioche. For large brioche divide the dough into 2 balls.

Lightly flour a flat surface. Roll out each small ball into a 4-inch circle or the large ball into a 10-inch circle. Prepare a baking sheet (18 x 13 x 1-inch) by lining it with parchment paper or buttering it. Place the dough circles on it, spacing each one 2 inches apart.

Cover the circles with a clean tea towel and let rise at room temperature in a draft-free location for 2 hours, or until 1 ½ times their original size.

Ardennaise Cake (suite)

Brioche Ardennaise

Preheat the oven to 325° about 15 minutes before baking.

When the dough has proofed, brush the top of each circle with the beaten egg using a pastry brush. Use your forefinger to poke 6 holes into the individual brioche or 12 holes into the large brioche circle. Pipe dollops of the filling into each of the holes in the brioche.

Immediately bake for 20 minutes or until golden brown.

Remove from the oven and brush the brioche with the glaze while the brioche are still warm.

Filling:

Make the filling while the dough is rising. In an electric mixer fitted with the whip attachment, combine the sugar and the softened butter and beat until creamy. Add the pastry cream and mix until well combined. Transfer filling to a pastry bag fitted with a plain tip. Alternatively, if you do not have a pastry bag, fill a heavy resealable plastic bag with the filling. Squeeze the air out before closing and cut a small hole in the bottom corner of the bag. Set aside in the refrigerator until ready to use.

Glaze:

Combine the sugar and water in a small bowl and whisk until the sugar dissolves. Use this glaze to brush on warm brioche.

See the illustrations in the glossary for further instructions on folding and shaping brioche dough.

Serves 8

Moderate

Filling

½ cup granulated sugar

4 tablespoons unsalted butter, softened

1 cup Pastry Cream
(see recipe page 104)

1 beaten egg for egg wash

Glaze

½ cup confectioners' sugar

2 tablespoons water

This is one of la Madeleine's first coffee cakes.

Crème Fraîche Coffee Cake

Gâteau à la Crème Fraîche

Ⓟ
Ⓟ
Ⓟ

Crème Fraîche Coffee Cake

6 tablespoons unsalted butter, softened

⅔ cup chopped pecans

1 cup light brown sugar

1 teaspoon natural vanilla extract

¾ cup granulated sugar

½ cup canola oil

2 eggs

2 cups all-purpose flour

1 tablespoon baking powder

1 teaspoon baking soda

¼ teaspoon salt

2 cups crème fraîche*

*Make crème fraîche by mixing ¾ cup of heavy whipping cream into 1¼ cups sour cream. Let stand for 3 hours or until thickened.

Crème Fraîche is sold in France instead of sour cream in the dairy section of the market. It's so popular it even comes in cans. This nutty, tangy cream is very versatile. It keeps longer than fresh cream and doesn't curdle when you cook with it. You can use it cold on fruit salads or mixed with herbs as a dip. Deglaze the pan after cooking chicken with vermouth and add some crème fraîche for an easy and delicious pan sauce. You can also make crème fraîche by combining 1 cup of heavy cream with 2 tablespoons of buttermilk, stir and let stand for 12 hours until thickened.

Requires some advance preparation.

Preheat the oven to 350°.

Butter a 12-cup bundt pan, preferably non-stick.

Using a fork, mix the butter, pecans and brown sugar together in a small bowl until crumbly. Set aside.

Combine the vanilla, sugar, oil and eggs in the bowl of an electric mixer fitted with the paddle attachment. Mix at medium speed until smooth.

In a separate bowl, sift the flour, baking powder, baking soda and salt together.

Add ⅓ of the flour mixture to the egg mixture, then ⅓ of the crème fraîche, mixing well after each addition. Continue adding the flour and then the crème fraîche alternately until well mixed.

Layer half the batter in the prepared baking pan, then ⅓ of the crumbs. Top with the remaining batter. Sprinkle the top with the remaining crumbs.

Place the pan into the oven and bake for 50 minutes or until a skewer inserted into the cake comes out moist but clean.

Cool the cake in the pan on a wire rack for 10 minutes. Loosen the edges of the cake with a sharp knife. Invert the cake onto the wire rack and let the cake cool completely. Slide the cake from the rack onto a serving plate.

Serves 10
Moderate

You can substitute sour cream for the crème fraîche.

Almond Cake
Le Pain de Gênes

This version of a traditional almond cake uses cornstarch instead of all-purpose flour for a rich, moist cake. Be sure to beat the eggs thoroughly after each addition; this is what gives the cake its lightness.

Preheat the oven to 325°.

Butter a 9 x 2-inch round cake pan, preferably non-stick. Sprinkle the sliced almonds over the butter. Shake the pan so there is a single layer of almonds coating the pan. Shake out the excess. Set pan aside.

Sift the cornstarch and the baking powder together in a small bowl. Set aside.

Place the ground almonds, confectioners' sugar and butter together in the bowl of an electric mixer fitted with the whip attachment. Beat at medium speed until well blended.

Add the eggs, one at a time, beating very well after each addition. Continue beating at medium speed. It should take 10 minutes to beat in the eggs.

Add the rum. Beat again to combine.

Using a spatula, fold in the reserved cornstarch and baking powder. Be sure to incorporate all of the cornstarch from the side of the bowl.

Pour the batter into the prepared baking pan. It should be no more than ⅔ full.

Bake for 50 minutes or until golden brown and baked through. Test the cake by inserting a toothpick in the center. The toothpick should come out moist but clean. The cake will be firm and not liquid. Add additional time if necessary.

Set the cake pan on a wire rack and let cool for 5 minutes. Loosen the edges of the cake with a sharp knife. Invert the cake onto the wire rack. Brush the top of the cake with the lavender honey or apricot jam while the cake is still warm.

Let the cake cool completely. Slide the cake from the rack onto a serving plate.

Makes 1 9-inch cake

Moderate

Ⓟ

Ⓟ

Ⓟ

Almond Cake

4 tablespoons almonds, sliced

⅓ cup cornstarch

1 teaspoon baking powder

2 cups finely ground almonds, without peel

2 cups confectioners' sugar

6 tablespoons unsalted butter, softened

4 eggs

2 teaspoons dark rum

¼ cup lavender honey or ½ cup apricot jam, melted over low heat

---

Try this cake with Raspberry Coulis and ice cream for dessert.

Lemon & Ginger Cake

Pain au Citron et Gingembre

This is a moist tea loaf bright with the flavor of lemon and ginger. Here's a tip for grating citrus zest: cover the zest side of your grater with plastic wrap and then grate the fruit. The zest will stay in the plastic wrap instead of the holes of the grater.

Cake:

Preheat the oven to 350°.

Butter and flour a loaf pan, preferably non-stick. Set aside.

Using an electric mixer fitted with the paddle attachment, mix the eggs, sugar, cream, salt, ginger and lemon zest together at medium speed for 5 minutes or until the mixture is thick and pale yellow.

In a separate bowl, sift together the flour and baking powder and add to the egg mixture.

Add the rum and melted butter, and then mix at low speed until just combined. Pour the batter into the prepared cake pan.

Place the pan in the oven and bake for 40 minutes or until golden brown on top and a toothpick inserted in the center comes out moist but clean. Remove the cake from the oven and set on a rack for 10 minutes to cool. Loosen the sides of the cake with a knife. Unmold the cake onto the rack and then flip it right side up.

Brush with the glaze while the cake is still warm so that the flavors are absorbed into the cake.

Glaze:

Mix the confectioners' sugar and lemon juice together in a small bowl until it is a spreadable consistency. Brush on the warm cake.

Serves 8
Easy

Ⓟ

Cake

3 eggs

¾ cup granulated sugar

⅛ cup heavy cream

pinch of salt

pinch of ginger

zest of 2 organic lemons

¾ cup all-purpose flour

2 teaspoons baking powder

2 tablespoons dark rum

4 tablespoons unsalted butter, melted

Glaze

⅓ cup confectioners' sugar

2 tablespoons freshly squeezed lemon juice

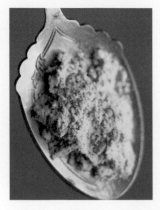

Serve with gently whipped cream flavored with vanilla and ginger.

Walnut & Dried Apricot Cake

Pain aux Noix et Abricots

This is our version of a traditional walnut cake from the Perigord region of France. It's a very moist, dense cake rich with the tang of apricots and the aroma of Cognac.

Cake

½ cup Cognac

1 cup pitted dried apricots, cut into ¼-inch pieces

9 tablespoons unsalted butter, softened

1 ¼ cups granulated sugar

5 eggs

⅔ cup ground almonds

⅔ cup all-purpose flour

½ teaspoon baking powder

additional Cognac to make 2 tablespoons

1 cup finely chopped walnuts

Glaze

⅓ cup confectioners' sugar

2 tablespoons Cognac

Cake:

Place the apricots in a small bowl and add the Cognac. Set aside at room temperature for 45 minutes to plump the apricots.

Preheat the oven to 350°.

Butter and flour a 9-inch cake pan, preferably non-stick.

Place the butter and sugar in the bowl of a mixer fitted with the whip attachment. Cream the mixture at medium speed until lighter in color and fluffy, about 5 minutes.

Add the eggs one at a time, beating well after each addition, scraping the bowl as necessary.

Add the ground almonds, flour and baking powder. Beat until smooth.

Drain the apricots and measure the amount of Cognac remaining. Add additional Cognac to make 2 tablespoons. Pour the Cognac, apricots and walnuts into the bowl and beat briefly again until well blended.

Pour the batter into the prepared cake pan.

Place the pan in the oven and bake for 45 minutes or until golden brown on top and a toothpick inserted in the center comes out moist but clean. Remove the cake from the oven and set on a rack for 5 minutes to cool. Loosen the sides of the cake with a knife. Unmold the cake onto the rack and then flip it right side up.

Brush with the glaze while the cake is still warm so that the flavors are absorbed into the cake.

Glaze:

Mix the confectioners' sugar and Cognac together in a small bowl until it is a spreadable consistency. Brush on the warm cake.

Makes 1 9-inch cake

Moderate

This cake freezes beautifully.

Almond Cookies
Financiers

These are crisp cookie-like cakes with a moist interior. You may want to make 2 batches, as these little cakes are addicting. They will keep up to a week in an airtight container. Be sure that the butter is still hot when you add it the egg mixture to ensure the right texture.

꩜

Preheat the oven to 350°.

Generously butter 12 financier molds. Refrigerate the molds until you are ready to bake the financiers.

Melt the 8 tablespoons butter in a small saucepan over medium heat. Leave the pan over the heat, watching all the time, until the butter turns a light caramel color and smells nutty. This is called "beurre noisette." Keep the butter warm until ready to use.

Using a food processor fitted with the metal blade, process the sugar and the almonds until very fine.

Place the nut mixture into a mixing bowl and stir in the flour.

Add the egg whites and vanilla and mix until just combined.

Pour the butter in a steady stream into the flour mixture and mix with a spatula until just combined.

Place the molds on a baking sheet. Fill the molds about ¾ full with the batter. Place the baking sheet into the oven and bake 18 to 20 minutes or until golden brown. Remove from the oven and cool on a wire rack 2 minutes before unmolding. Cool completely on the rack.

Makes 24

Moderate

ⓟ
ⓟ
ⓟ

Almond Cookies

butter for the molds, softened

8 tablespoons unsalted butter

¾ cup granulated sugar

scant ½ cup almonds, slivered

½ cup all-purpose flour

4 egg whites, at room temperature

½ teaspoon natural vanilla extract

Use mini muffin tins if you can't find financier molds.

Cranberry Pecan Scones

Cranberry Pecan Scones

3 cups all-purpose flour

⅓ cup granulated sugar

3 teaspoons baking powder

1 teaspoon salt

½ teaspoon baking soda

1 ½ cups (12 ounces) unsalted butter, softened and cut into ½-inch pieces

¾ cup dried cranberries

½ cup pecan pieces

¾ cup buttermilk

1 egg, beaten

8 teaspoons granulated sugar

crème fraîche as an accompaniment, optional

Cranberry Pecan Scones

Scones aux Canneberges et Noix de Pécan

We know scones aren't very French, but these are so popular at la Madeleine we had to include them. This dough is very rich and crumbly so don't be tempted to overmix. These scones will be large but they will soon disappear.

Preheat the oven to 400°.

Line a baking sheet about 18 x 13 x 1-inch (or 2 smaller ones) with parchment paper. Set aside.

Combine the flour, sugar, baking powder, salt and baking soda together in the bowl of an electric mixer fitted with the paddle attachment. Add the butter and mix at low speed until the mixture resembles coarse meal. Watch carefully because this happens very fast, about 30 to 45 seconds. Add the cranberries and the pecans and mix about 5 seconds, or just long enough to distribute the cranberries and pecans. Remove the bowl from the mixer. Using a fork, slowly add the buttermilk, stirring with the fork to make a soft dough. Do not overmix. The mixture will be crumbly, not smooth. This step in the mixing is important because the crumbly mixture will result in tender, flaky scones.

Turn the dough onto a lightly floured surface. Form the dough into a round shape about 9 inches in diameter and 1 inch thick. Cut the dough into 8 wedges with a sharp knife or pizza cutter. Place the wedges on the prepared baking sheet, about 2 inches apart.

Using a pastry brush, brush the tops of the scones lightly with the egg and sprinkle each scone with 1 teaspoon of granulated sugar.

Place the scones in the oven and bake for 12 minutes, then reduce the heat to 350°. Bake for 12 more minutes or until the scones are golden brown. Let the scones cool for 10 minutes on the baking sheet.

Serve with the scones with jam and crème fraîche if desired.

Makes 8 large scones

Moderate

 Try these with apricots and white chocolate chips.

Blueberry Muffins

Petits Gâteaux aux Myrtilles

This recipe is a little different from your typical muffin recipe. It is a variation of the cake with blueberries served at Lenôtre, a famous Parisian bakery. This is the recipe we use for blueberry muffins at la Madeleine.

Preheat the oven to 325°.

Butter enough muffin tins to hold 18 muffins or line the muffin tins with paper muffin cups. Set aside.

Cream the butter and sugar together in an electric mixer fitted with the paddle attachment until light and fluffy, about 5 minutes.

Add the eggs, one at a time, beating well after each addition. Scrape the sides of the bowl as necessary. Add the vanilla. Beat again and remove the bowl from the mixer.

In another bowl, combine the flour, salt and baking powder together. Using a wooden spoon or a spatula, carefully fold the flour mixture into the creamed mixture until just combined. The batter will seem coarse. Do not overmix the batter. Add the blueberries and stir briefly to distribute. Fill the muffin cups ¾ full.

Place the muffins in the oven and bake for 30 minutes or until puffed and light golden brown. Remove them from the oven and place on a wire rack to cool for 10 minutes. Remove the muffins from the tin by turning out, loosening the sides with a knife if necessary. Finish cooling on the rack.

Makes 18 muffins

Moderate

Blueberry Muffins

12 tablespoons unsalted butter, softened

1 cup granulated sugar

5 eggs

1 teaspoon natural vanilla extract

2 ½ cups all-purpose flour

1 teaspoon salt

1 tablespoon baking powder

2 cups (1 pint) fresh blueberries, dusted with flour

Flour the berries so they won't sink to the bottom of the muffins.

Doughnuts

Doughnuts

4 cups bread flour

½ cup granulated sugar

1 teaspoon salt

2 tablespoons unsalted butter, softened

3 eggs

1 cup milk

1 package (¼ ounce) dry fast-rising yeast

4 –6 cups canola oil for frying

1 cup granulated sugar

2 teaspoons ground cinnamon

Beignets

Beignets are usually sold in France during the two weeks before or during Carnaval. The task of frying beignets falls to the apprentice bakers. This is a big job when you have to make enough to feed an entire village!

Combine the flour, ½ cup sugar, salt, butter, eggs and milk in the bowl of an electric mixer fitted with the dough hook. Start the mixer at low speed. After the mixture begins to combine, sprinkle in the yeast and continue mixing. When the flour is absorbed, increase the speed to medium and beat until the dough forms a ball and leaves the side of the bowl, about 10 to 15 minutes. Pay attention to the mixer during this time since it may move about on the counter. Remove the dough from the bowl and knead the dough on a smooth surface. Add a tiny bit of flour if necessary to form a soft dough. Form into a ball, lightly dust with flour and place into a large bowl. Cover with plastic wrap and set aside in a warm place until doubled in size, about 2 hours.

When the dough has risen use a dough scraper to remove the dough from the bowl. Lightly flour a smooth surface and gently knead the dough. Pat the dough into a rectangle about 14 x 12 x 1-inch. Use a very sharp knife or a pizza cutter to cut the dough into 20 squares. Leave the dough in squares or roll each square into a ball. Line a baking sheet with a tea towel and sprinkle with flour. Place each piece of dough on the towel, allowing 2 inches between each one so they do not touch when risen. Cover with an additional tea towel and let the dough rest at room temperature for 1 ½ hours or until doubled in size.

While the dough is rising pour the oil into a deep pot or a deep fat fryer to a depth of about 4 inches. About 20 minutes before frying, heat the oil to a temperature of 365° to 375°. Check the temperature with a thermometer.

Fry the beignets, a few at a time, until golden brown on both sides, about 6 minutes total. Turn the beignets so they cook twice on both sides. Once the beignets are cooked remove them with a slotted spoon or skimmer and drain on a wire rack. Repeat frying until they are all cooked. Adjust the heat as needed to maintain a steady temperature.

Mix the sugar and cinnamon together on a large flat plate. Roll each of the beignets in the cinnamon sugar while still warm and serve right away.

Makes 20 beignets

Moderate

Beignets are simply pieces of brioche dough fried until warm and crisp.

Croissant Dough

Pâte à Croissant

Croissant Dough

3 ½ cups bread flour

2 teaspoons salt

¼ cup granulated sugar

1 package (¼ ounce) dry
fast-rising yeast

¼ cup (¼ of an 8-ounce package)
Keller's European Style Butter, softened

2 eggs

1 cup milk

¾ cup (¾ of an 8 ounce package)
Keller's European Style Butter, cold

1 egg for egg wash

Croissants are not easy to make at home and it is imperative that you use bread flour with its higher gluten content and French-style butter. We have found that Keller's European Style Butter works the best in this recipe and it is readily available at most large grocery stores. It is important to add enough milk to make the dough combine easily; but if you add too much your dough will be sticky and hard to manage. It may take several attempts to make the perfect croissant.

Requires overnight preparation.

Combine the flour, salt and sugar in the bowl of an electric mixer fitted with the dough hook attachment. Mix briefly at low speed, about 1 minute, to blend. Add the yeast, the ¼ cup of softened butter and the eggs and mix at low speed. Immediately add the milk slowly, adding only enough to make the dough combine. Scrape the sides of the bowl as needed.

Mix at low speed for 5 minutes.

Increase the speed to medium and mix for 10 more minutes or until the dough forms a smooth ball around the hook. Check the machine from time to time to make sure it does not "walk" during the kneading.

Remove the dough from the mixer and place into a square, approximately 10 x 10-inch plastic container. Pat the dough into the corners; it may retract but will later rise to fill the container. Let the dough rest overnight in the refrigerator. The dough will expand somewhat because of the yeast.

When ready to shape the dough, remove the cold butter from the refrigerator. Lightly flour the butter and flatten it with a rolling pin. Continue pounding the butter with a rolling pin until it is pliable, almost the same texture as the croissant dough. Shape the butter into a 6 x 5-inch rectangle.

Croissant Dough (suite)

Pâte à Croissant

Remove the dough from the refrigerator and place onto a lightly floured flat surface. Roll into an 8 x 12-inch rectangle. Place the rolled butter on the top half of the dough rectangle, leaving a 1-inch border. Fold the unbuttered dough over the butter and press the edges together to form a seal. The butter will be covered with the dough.

Roll the dough from left to right to layer in the butter.

Roll out the dough and form a rectangle 10 x 26 inches. Work quickly and keep dusting your work surface with flour. After the dough is rolled out, fold the dough in thirds like a letter. This is one "turn." Cover the dough with plastic wrap and refrigerate for 1 hour. During this time the dough will relax and the butter will become hard again. It is important to keep the butter cold so that it stays separate from the dough. This separation is what will produce the flaky layers in the croissant.

After 1 hour, remove the dough from the refrigerator and roll out the dough again into a 10 x 26-inch rectangle. Then fold into thirds. This is the second "turn." After the second "turn" place the dough into the refrigerator again for 1 hour. It is then ready to be rolled and shaped as desired.

See the illustrations in the glossary for further instructions on folding and shaping croissant dough.

Difficult

Makes about 1 ¾ pounds of croissant dough

This dough is the base for many breakfast goodies.

Chocolate Croissant

1 recipe Croissant Dough
(see recipe page 100)

6 ounces semi sweet chocolate chips,
preferably European

1 egg

Chocolate Croissant

Pain au Chocolat

This chocolate-filled roll is one of the best-sellers at la Madeleine. If you are going to the trouble of making these at home, make sure you use the very best chocolate you can find. European chocolate has a higher flavor profile than American chocolate and will really make a difference in this pastry.

Requires overnight preparation.

Croissant Dough:

The croissant dough should have had 2 "turns" and should have chilled in the refrigerator again for at least 1 hour before you begin preparation of this recipe.

Cover 2 baking sheets 18 x 13 x 1-inch with parchment paper and set aside.

Lightly flour a large flat surface. Roll out the croissant dough to form an 18 x 20-inch rectangle. If the dough become difficult to roll or the butter begins to melt, return the dough to the refrigerator and chill for 30 minutes. When the dough has rested, continue with the rolling.

Cut the dough into 3, 6-inch rectangles, then cut each rectangle into 4, 5-inch squares.

Place 2 teaspoons of the chocolate chips in the center of each square. Roll the dough like a jellyroll with the seam on the bottom. Flatten the roll slightly with your hand.

Place the rolls on the prepared baking sheet and cover with a damp cloth. Set aside to rise at room temperature in a draft-free location until doubled in volume, about 45 minutes.

Preheat the oven to 375° about 15 minutes before baking.

When the rolls are ready to bake beat the egg with a fork and a pinch of salt. Gently brush the tops of the rolls with the beaten egg.

Place the baking pan in the oven and bake for 25 to 30 minutes or until golden brown.

Let the rolls cool on a wire rack.

See the illustrations in the glossary for further instructions on folding and shaping croissant dough.

Makes 12 Chocolate Croissants

Croissant dough difficult, shaping easy

Adding a pinch of salt to the egg wash makes the egg blend better.

𝒫

Pain Raisin

Pain Raisin

Pain Raisin

1 cup golden raisins

3 tablespoons dark rum

¼ cup water

Pastry Cream

½ cup granulated sugar, divided use

2 cups milk

4 tablespoons cornstarch

4 egg yolks

4 tablespoons unsalted butter

1 teaspoon natural vanilla extract

1 recipe Croissant Dough
(see recipe page 100)

Glaze

⅓ cup confectioners' sugar

2 tablespoons water

This is another breakfast treat that you may want to enjoy at la Madeleine. The croissant dough is the hardest part; the raisins and the pastry cream are easy to prepare. The shaping is also simple; you just roll up the dough like a jellyroll. In France, Pain Raisin are often available in two versions. One is made from croissant dough at the boulangerie and another from brioche dough at the Pâtisserie. Both versions are delicious!

Requires overnight preparation.

Raisins:

Combine the raisins, rum and water in a small bowl. Cover and let macerate and plump overnight in the refrigerator.

Pastry Cream:

Put ¼ cup of the sugar in a medium saucepan. Add the milk and stir to combine. Place the pan over high heat and bring to a boil while stirring occasionally.

In a separate mixing bowl, combine the remaining ¼ cup sugar and the cornstarch. Add the egg yolks and mix well with a whisk. The mixture should be well combined and fairly thick.

Once the milk is boiling, pour one-fourth of the milk into the egg mixture to equalize the temperature, stirring constantly. Reduce the heat to medium-low. Pour the egg mixture into the rest of the milk and return to the heat, whisking to combine and distribute the heat. Cook until the cream thickens and comes to a full boil. Boil for about 1 minute.

Remove from the heat, add the butter and vanilla, and stir until the butter melts. Pour the cream into a shallow bowl and cover with plastic wrap, allowing the plastic to touch the surface of the custard. If not using immediately, store in an airtight container in the refrigerator.

Use this pastry cream in fruit tarts and other treats.

Pain Raisin (suite)

Pain Raisin

Croissant Dough:

The croissant dough should have had 2 "turns" and should have chilled in the refrigerator again for at least 1 hour before you begin preparation of this recipe.

Cover 2 baking sheets 18 x 13 x 1-inch with parchment paper and set aside.

Lightly flour a large flat surface. Roll out the croissant dough to form a sheet approximately 26 inches long and 16 inches wide. If the dough becomes difficult to roll or the butter begins to melt, return the dough to the refrigerator and let it relax for 30 minutes. When the dough has rested, continue with the rolling.

Spread the cooled pastry cream evenly over the dough leaving a 1-inch border at the edges of the dough without cream.

Sprinkle with the raisins and any of the liquid that is not absorbed.

Roll tightly lengthwise like a jellyroll.

Cut the rolled dough into 1 ¼-inch slices and place the slices on the prepared baking sheets about 2 inches apart. Tuck in any ends that come undone during the transfer. Let the slices rise at room temperature in a draft-free location for 3 hours or until the dough is 1½ times its original size. The rolls will be about 3 to 4 inches across.

Preheat the oven to 350° about 15 minutes before baking.

Bake for 20 minutes or until golden brown.

As soon as the rolls come out of the oven, brush the tops with the glaze.

Glaze:

Combine the sugar and water in a small bowl and whisk until the sugar dissolves. Use the glaze to brush on warm pastries.

See the illustrations in the glossary for further instructions on folding and shaping croissant dough.

Makes 16 Raisin Croissant Rolls

Croissant dough difficult, shaping moderate

Flan Pretzel

1 recipe Croissant Dough
(see recipe page 100)

1 recipe Pastry Cream
(see recipe page 104)

Glaze

⅓ cup confectioners' sugar

2 tablespoons water

Croissant Pretzel

Flan Pretzel

Legend has it that the first pretzels were invented by a French monk who twisted some extra bread dough into a shape resembling children at prayer. These pretzels, made with buttery croissant dough and filled with pastry cream, are found in Alsacian pastry shops.

Requires overnight preparation.

The croissant dough should have had 2 "turns" and should have chilled in the refrigerator again for at least 1 hour before you begin preparation of this recipe.

Cover 2 baking sheets 18 x 13 x 1-inch with parchment paper and set aside.

Lightly flour a large flat surface. Roll out the croissant dough to form a sheet approximately 24 inches long and 18 inches wide. If the dough becomes difficult to roll or the butter begins to melt, return the dough to the refrigerator to relax for 30 minutes. When the dough has rested, continue with the rolling.

Cut the dough lengthwise into 1-inch strips. You should have 18 dough strips.

Roll and twist each individual strip again into a 24-inch length (when you pick up the dough, or move it, it will shrink somewhat in length).

Make a big circle with the twisted strip and twist at the bottom, leaving about 2 inches of the ends loose. Twist again and fold the ends up to form a pretzel.

Place each pretzel as formed on the prepared baking about 2 inches apart.

Let the pretzels rise at room temperature in a draft-free location for 2 hours or until doubled in size.

Preheat the oven to 350° about 15 minutes before baking.

Using a pastry bag with a smooth tip, fill each section of the pretzel with pastry cream. Alternatively, if you do not have a pastry bag, fill a heavy resealable plastic bag. Squeeze the air out before closing and cut a small hole in the bottom corner of the bag.

Place the pretzels in the oven and bake for 20 minutes or until golden brown.

As soon as the pretzels come out of the oven, brush the tops with the glaze.

Cool to room temperature.

Glaze:

Combine the sugar and the water in a small bowl and whisk until the sugar dissolves. Use this glaze to brush on warm pastries.

See the illustrations in the glossary for further instructions on folding and shaping croissant dough.

Makes 18 Croissant Pretzels. Croissant dough difficult, shaping moderate.

roissants

Croissants

In the summer of 1693, the Turkish army lay siege to the Austrian capital of Vienna. Meeting with heavy opposition, the Turks decided to tunnel under the city walls and defeat the Austrians. The bakers of the city, working as usual in the middle of the night, heard the digging and sounded the alarm. The city was saved and by the autumn the Turkish army was defeated. In honor of the alert bakers, the croissant was created, its crescent shape recalling the flag of the defeated Turkish army.

The croissant dough should have had 2 "turns" and should have chilled in the refrigerator again for at least 1 hour before you begin preparation of this recipe.

Cover 2 baking sheets 18 x 13 x 1-inch with parchment paper and set aside.

Place the cold dough on a lightly floured flat surface. Roll out the dough into a rectangle about 16 inches long by 24 inches wide. If the dough becomes difficult to roll or the butter begins to melt, return the dough to the refrigerator to relax for 30 minutes. You may have to return the dough to the refrigerator several times. When the dough is the correct size, cut the dough in half, then in half again. Cut each square into triangles 5 inches across on the wide side. Cut a notch in the middle of the wide side for ease in shaping. Roll the dough into a crescent, starting with the wide side. Fold the "tail" under.

Place the croissants on a baking sheet lined with parchment paper and set aside in a warm draft-free location to rise for about 1 ½ hours or until doubled in volume.

Preheat the oven to 375°.

Just before baking gently brush each croissant with a beaten egg (egg wash). Place in the oven and bake for 15 minutes or until golden brown on top.

See the illustrations in the glossary for further instructions on folding and shaping croissant dough.

Makes 16 croissants

Difficult

You may want to visit your neighborhood la Madeleine to enjoy this treat.

Croissants

1 recipe Croissant Dough
(see recipe page 100)

1 egg

1 tablespoon granulated sugar

1 teaspoon cornstarch

2 cups fresh cherries, pitted

4 eggs

pinch of salt

½ cup granulated sugar

⅓ cup all-purpose flour

1 cup whole milk

4 tablespoons unsalted butter, melted

1 teaspoon grated lemon peel

1 teaspoon natural vanilla extract

1 teaspoon Grand Marnier

confectioners' sugar

Cherry Custard

Clafoutis aux Cerises

This custardy fruit dessert is a traditional farmhouse favorite. You can use different fruits, depending on the season, like apricots, apples, plums or pears. Try topping the custard with crème fraîche or whipped cream. You can also sprinkle with more Grand Marnier while the custard is still warm to further enhance the flavor.

Preheat the oven to 325°.

Butter a 1 ½-quart shallow baking dish, preferably ceramic or glass.

Mix the 1 tablespoon granulated sugar and the cornstarch together in a small bowl.

Place the cherries in a medium bowl and toss with the sugar mixture until the cherries are coated. Arrange the cherries on the bottom of the prepared baking dish. Set aside.

Whisk the eggs, salt and the ½ cup of granulated sugar together in a large mixing bowl. Add the flour and mix well. Then add the milk, butter, lemon peel, vanilla and the Grand Marnier. Whisk until smooth and pour over the cherries.

Place the pan in the oven and bake for 55 minutes or until golden brown and set in the center. Cool slightly and dust with confectioners' sugar. Serve warm.

Serves 6

Easy

Place confectioners' sugar in a sieve and shake to evenly dust baked goods.

Les Notes

Conversion Chart

U.S. Weights & Measures

1 pinch = less than 1/8 teaspoon (dry)

1 dash = 3 drops to 1/4 teaspoon (liquid)

3 teaspoons = 1 tablespoon = 1/2 ounce (liquid and dry)

2 tablespoons = 1 ounce (liquid and dry)

4 tablespoons = 2 ounces (liquid and dry) = 1/4 cup

5 1/3 tablespoons = 1/3 cup

16 tablespoons = 48 teaspoons

32 tablespoons = 16 ounces = 2 cups = 1 pound

64 tablespoons = 32 ounces (liquid) = 1 quart = 2 pounds

1 cup = 8 ounces (liquid) = 1/2 pint

2 cups = 16 ounces (liquid) = 1 pint

4 cups = 32 ounces (liquid) = 2 pints = 1 quart

16 cups = 128 ounces (liquid) = 4 quarts = 1 gallon

1 quart = 2 pints (dry)

8 quarts = 1 peck (dry)

4 pecks = 1 bushel (dry)

Approximate Equivalents

1 quart (liquid) = about 1 liter

8 tablespoons = 4 ounces = 1/2 cup = 1 stick butter

1 cup all-purpose presifted flour = 5 ounces

1 cup stoneground yellow cornmeal = 4 1/2 ounces

1 cup granulated sugar = 8 ounces

1 cup brown sugar = 6 ounces

1 cup confectioners' sugar = 4 1/2 ounces

1 large egg = 2 ounces = 1/4 cup = 4 tablespoons

1 egg yolk = 1 tablespoon +1 teaspoon

1 egg white = 2 tablespoons + 2 teaspoons

3/4 cup ground almonds = 4 ounces

3 cups peeled & sliced apples = 1 pound whole apples

1/3 diced bacon = 2 ounces

1/2 cup lightly packed grated cheese = 2 ounces

3/4 cup raisins = 4 ounces

Conversion Chart (suite)

Temperatures

° Fahrenheit (F) to ° Celsius (C)

-10° F = -23.3°C (freezer storage)
0° F = -17.7° C
32° F = 0° C (water freezes)
50° F = 10° C
68° F = 20° C
100° F = 37.7° C
150° F = 65.5° C
205° F = 96.1°C (water simmers)
212° F = 100° C (water boils)
300° F = 148.8° C
325° F = 162.8°C
350° F = 177° C (baking)
375° F = 190.5° C
400° F = 204.4° C (hot oven)
425° F = 218.3° C
450° F = 232° C (very hot oven)
475° F = 246.1° C
500° F = 260° C (broiling)

Conversion Factors

If you need to convert measurements into their equivalents in another system, here's how to do it.

Weight
ounces to grams: ounce x 28.3 = grams
grams to ounces: gram x 0.0353 = ounces
pounds to grams: pound x 453.59 = grams
pounds to kilograms: pound x .045 = kilograms

Liquid Measures
ounces to milliliters: ounce x 30 = milliliters
cups to liters: cup x 0.24 = liters

Temperatures
Fahrenheit (°F) to Celsius (°C): $[(F-32) \times 5] \div 9 = C$
Celsius (°C) to Fahrenheit (°F): $[(C \times 9) \div 5] + 32 = F$

Dimensions
inches to centimeters: inch x 2.54 = centimeters
centimeters to inches: centimeters x 0.39 = inches

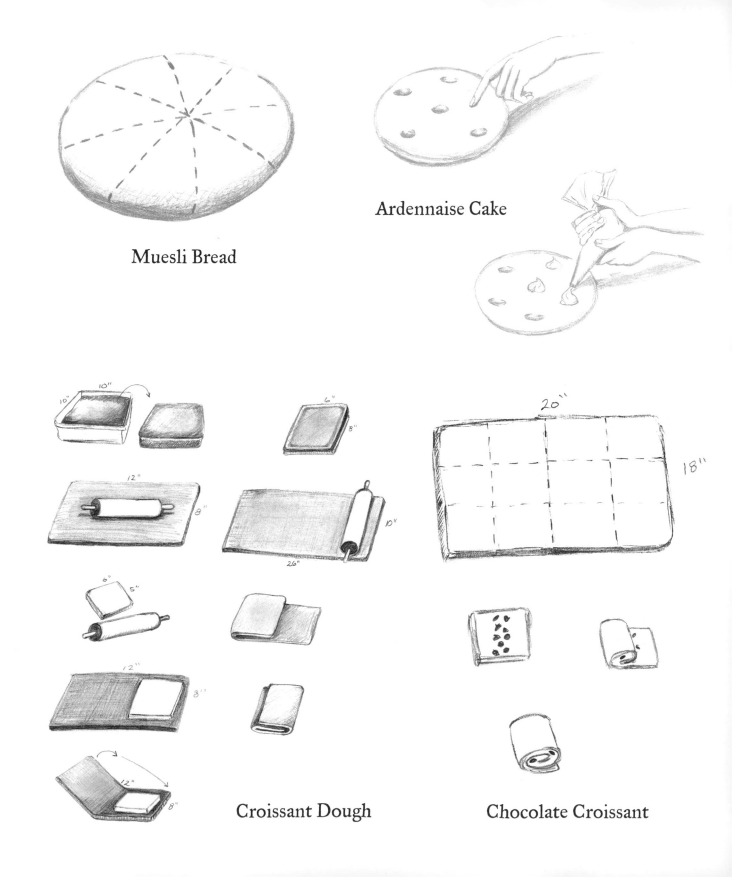

Muesli Bread

Ardennaise Cake

Croissant Dough

Chocolate Croissant

26"

16"

24"

16"

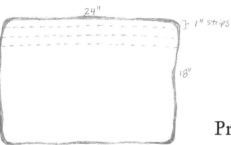

Pain Raisin

24"

7 1" strips

18"

Twist
each
strip

Pretzel Croissants

Croissants

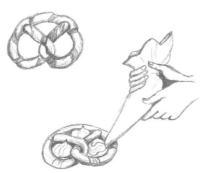

Glossary

Angostura Bitters	a blend of herbs used to flavor drinks and as a "digestive"
Baguette	a long cylindrical French loaf with a crisp brown crust and a chewy interior
Béarnaise	a hot creamy sauce made with vinegar, wine, tarragon and shallots; finished with butter and egg yolks
Béchamel Sauce	a basic French white sauce made with flour, butter and milk
Beurre Blanc	a thick smooth sauce made from vinegar, white wine, shallots and chilled butter
Beurre Manié	a paste made of softened butter and flour, used to thicken sauces
Beurre Noisette	butter gently heated until it becomes brown in color and nutty in taste
Boursin	a triple cream cheese flavored with herbs
Bread Flour	a high-gluten blend of hard wheat flour, malted barley and vitamin C
Brie	a soft creamy cow's milk cheese with an edible rind
Brioche	light yeast bread made with eggs and butter
Brut	the driest variety of Champagne
Buckwheat	a cereal plant that yields a gray flour, used in France to make crêpes
Café au Lait	equal amounts of scalded milk and coffee
Calvados	a brandy made from apple cider in the Calvados region of France
Canola Oil	a bland oil used in cooking; has a low saturated fat level
Caramelize	to heat sugar under a broiler until it melts and browns
Chanterelle	a trumpet-shaped wild mushroom known for its delicate flavor
Chiffonade	thin strips or shreds of herbs or vegetables
Cognac	a French brandy, aged at least 3 years
Comté	a cow's milk cheese from Franche-Comté; also known as Comté Gruyère
Coulis	a thick purée or sauce
Crème Frâiche	a thickened heavy cream with a nutty flavor
Crêpe Pan	a shallow flat-bottomed frying pan
Double Boiler	2 pots that fit together; the lower pot is filled with simmering water, which heats the contents of the upper pot
Dough Scraper	a small, hard plastic scraper that fits in your hand and cleans all the dough from a bowl
Egg Wash	a mixture of egg and water brushed over baked goods to give them a glossy sheen
Fold	combine a light airy mixture like egg whites with a heavier mixture, using a down-across-and-over motion

French Butter	has less water content than American butter; is always unsalted
Ginger root	the root of the ginger plant; peel and use when fresh ginger is called for in a recipe
Glaze	a thin glossy coating for hot or cold foods
Grand Marnier	one of France's most renowned liquors, made from the dried peel of green oranges from the West Indies
Grapefruit Knife	a small knife with a curved, flexible blade that is serrated on both sides
Gruyère	a French cheese made from unpasteurized cow's milk, known for its smooth flavor and nutty finish
Half & Half	equal parts of light cream and milk
Heavy Cream	cream with a fat content of 36% to 40%, it will double in volume when whipped
Herbes de Provence	a blend of dry herbs from the South of France, usually including basil, fennel seed, lavender, marjoram, rosemary, sage and thyme
Jambon de Bayonne	a dried and smoked ham from the Bayonne region of France
Kirsch	a clear cherry brandy
Knead	to press dough with your hands, folding and refolding to make it smooth and elastic
Kugelhopf	a light yeast bread from Alsace
Lavender Honey	honey made from lavender flowers
Lillet	a French apéritif made from wine, brandy and fruits
Macerate	to put food in a liquid to tenderize and absorb flavors, especially fruits
Morel	an earthy, smoky-flavored wild mushroom
Muesli	a cereal mixture of oats, fruits and milk
Muesli Bread	bread made from dried muesli flakes
Navel Orange	a seedless sweet orange
Nutella	a blend of hazelnut paste and chocolate
Orange Flower Water	a flavoring for baked goods made from bitter-orange blossoms
Organic Food	grown without the use of any chemicals including fertilizers or pesticides
Parchment Paper	a specially developed grease and moisture-resistant paper used to line pans before baking
Passion Fruit	a tropical fruit of the passionflower plant
Pastry Bag	a reinforced bag rolled into a conical shape and holding a small stainless steel tip at the end; used to decorate or fill baked goods
Pectin	a natural gelatin-like substance used to thicken jams, jellies and preserves
Pernod	French liquor made from aniseed
Pie Weights	small pellet-like ceramic or metal weights used to keep a piecrust from shrinking
Piperade	a Basque specialty of cooked tomatoes and sweet peppers
Pith	the soft white layer between the outer peel and the flesh of citrus fruit

Porcini	also called cèpes, a fresh or dried wild mushroom
Portabello	an extremely large brown mushroom with a meaty texture
Prosciutto	a salt-cured, air-dried ham
Proof	dissolve yeast in a warm liquid until it bubbles; tests that the yeast is alive
Rock Sugar	amber-colored sugar crystals
Ruby Red Grapefruit	an exceptionally sweet variety of pink grapefruit
Runnel	the indentation at the bottom of a Kugelhopf mold
Scald	to cook a liquid over low heat just until it reaches the boiling point
Sea Salt	evaporated crystals from seawater; sea salt is said to be purer than table salt since it contains no additives
Seven Grain Bread	a whole-grain bread made with sesame seeds, millet and oat flakes
Shallot	a small variety of onion tinged with garlic flavor
Shitake	a meaty dark brown mushroom
Simmer	to cook food gently in a liquid heated to about 185°
Tart Pan	a round fluted ring with a removable bottom
Tart Shell	a freestanding mold or shell used to hold pie or quiche filling
Tawny Port	an aged, sweet fortified wine from Portugal
Temper	to equalize the temperature by adding a small amount of a hot ingredient to a cooler one
Tisane	an herbal tea
Truffles	a pungent fungus with a wrinkled skin that grows near the roots of trees
Turn	to fold and shape croissant dough
Vanilla Bean	the seedpod of a tropical orchid using in flavoring desserts
Vache Qui Rit	Laughing Cow processed cheese
Vermouth	a fortified white wine flavored with herbs and spices
Zest	outermost exterior peel of citrus fruit; usually oranges or lemons

Index